Soviet Nuclear Policy under Gorbachev

SOVIET NUCLEAR POLICY UNDER GORBACHEV

A Policy of Disarmament

DANIEL CALINGAERT

PRAEGER

New York
Westport, Connecticut
London

Library of Congress Cataloging-in-Publication Data

Calingaert, Daniel.
  Soviet nuclear policy under Gorbachev : a policy of disarmament /
  Daniel Calingaert.
    p.   cm.
  Includes bibliographical references and index.
  ISBN 0-275-93737-2 (alk. paper)
  1. Soviet Union—Military policy. 2. Nuclear disarmament—Soviet
Union.   I. Title.
UA770.C35   1991
327.1'74'0947—dc20   90-23452

British Library Cataloguing in Publication Data is available.

Copyright © 1991 by Daniel Calingaert

All rights reserved. No portion of this book may
be reproduced, by any process or technique, without
the express written consent of the publisher.

Library of Congress Catalog Card Number: 90-23452
ISBN: 0-275-93737-2

First published in 1991

Praeger Publishers, One Madison Avenue, New York, NY   10010
An imprint of Greenwood Publishing Group, Inc.

Printed in the United States of America

The paper used in this book complies with the
Permanent Paper Standard issued by the National
Information Standards Organization (Z39.48-1984).

10 9 8 7 6 5 4 3 2 1

To my parents,
with great affection

CONTENTS

Preface ix

Introduction 1

1 Innovation in Policy Formation 11

    Maneuvering in the Leadership 12
    Curtailing the Military's Influence 17
    Civilians Master Defense Policy 20

2 Economic Inducements for Disarmament 29

    Growth and Reform 30
    Easing the Defense Burden 34
    Savings from Arms Control 39

3 New Thinking on National Security Aims 47

    Defining National Interests 48
    Assessing the Threat 56
    Protecting Soviet Security 60

4	***Changes in Nuclear Strategy***	75
	Blocking Strategic Defense	76
	Competing Strategies	79
	Force Structures	83
	Weapons in Europe	87
5	***The Diplomacy of Arms Control***	99
	Reassessing Past Policy	100
	Improving Superpower Relations	102
	Restructuring European Security	112
6	***Soviet Conduct of Nuclear Arms Talks***	135
	Nuclear Disarmament in Europe	136
	Strategic Arms Cuts	143
	Control of Space Weapons	150
7	***Conclusion***	159
Glossary		165
Selected Bibliography		167
Index		173

PREFACE

This book explores the engines of rapid and profound change in Soviet nuclear arms control policy since 1985. The Gorbachev leadership replaced arms limitation with a fundamentally new policy of nuclear disarmament to assist the grand effort to align Soviet power with the world revolution in information technology. Weapons cuts provided an important instrument for forging an opening to the West, reducing the military component of Soviet security, and stimulating domestic reconstruction. By diverting resources to industrial modernization, restructuring the armed forces, and joining the global economy, Gorbachev and his supporters aim to revitalize Soviet economic strength and to exert renewed influence on international affairs.

The book offers a more systematic interpretation than hitherto attempted of Soviet nuclear arms control policy under Gorbachev. It examines the interaction among the various political, economic, and military sources of Soviet behavior to identify the aims and priorities underlying the Soviet pursuit of nuclear disarmament. It strives for analytical precision, attributing a particular cause for, or distinguishing primary from secondary motives behind, each Soviet action. The study assesses the range of factors steering Soviet policy to determine which of the contradictory objectives takes precedence in a given situation and how compatible Soviet goals reinforce each other. It shows how the outlook of Gorbachev and his advisors sets the course of Soviet actions and produces specific decisions. It illustrates the way that the Gorbachev leadership's priorities, embodied in new thinking, shape Soviet defense and foreign policies, which in turn govern Soviet conduct in negotiations on nuclear disarmament.

The Institute for the Study of World Politics, the RAND Corporation, and the Johns Hopkins School of Advanced International Studies provided financial and institutional support for my research. The manuscript was diligently edited by Bert Yaeger. Caroline Kennedy, Bruce Parrott, and Alex Pravda offered constructive criticism on an earlier draft. Robert O'Neill deserves a special thanks for his encouragement and for meticulously going through more drafts than is salutary.

INTRODUCTION

The Soviet Union under Gorbachev has embarked on a fundamentally new policy of nuclear disarmament. The pursuit of arms limitation has been replaced by arms reduction. Control of nuclear weapons in the 1970s and early 1980s merely regulated superpower rivalry. The first Strategic Arms Limitation Treaty (SALT I) imposed ceilings on an approximate balance in the number of weapons, and SALT II codified parity in nuclear potentials. In contrast, the USSR is now collaborating with the United States to make substantial cuts in nuclear stockpiles, to eliminate certain categories of weapons, and to restructure Soviet nuclear forces.

Before Gorbachev's accession, the Soviet Union insisted on preserving its newly acquired advantages in theater nuclear weapons, opposed significant cuts in its strategic arsenal, and refused to allow any research into space-based defenses. By 1990, the USSR was eliminating all of its intermediate- and short-range missiles, pressing for reduction of tactical nuclear weapons, agreeing to substantial cuts in strategic arms and intercontinental land-based missiles, and permitting some research and testing related to space weapons. Rather than seeking to protect Soviet gains, the Gorbachev leadership entered negotiations in order to restrain competition in nuclear arms. It made the bulk of the concessions and relinquished some of its advantages to reach agreement with the United States. Whereas the Brezhnev Politburo used arms control to collect the political dividends of its nuclear weapons buildup, Gorbachev and his associates engage in nuclear disarmament to shift from unilateral military to cooperative political means of achieving security.

The Gorbachev leadership has pursued a policy of nuclear disarmament as part of its grand effort to reconstitute the sources and exercise of Soviet power in line with the "scientific-technological revolution." It has radically altered the Soviet approach to arms control to promote its fundamental aim of modernizing the Soviet system and transforming the USSR's role in world affairs. Gorbachev and fellow reformers have set out to establish an efficient economy and dynamic society and thereby to exert influence abroad. Accordingly, they seek to establish cooperative relations with the West, to reduce military priorities, and to render the Soviet armed forces technologically competitive.

The proponents of *perestroika* measure power primarily by the strength of Soviet productive capacity and the quality of Soviet life. They understand that power in today's world is derived from the acquisition and effective management of advanced technology, so they are determined to lead the Soviet Union into the scientific-technological revolution. The creation of sophisticated information-processing systems, their diffusion throughout the economy and application to the production of goods and provision of services, boosts the USSR's capacity to furnish material benefits to its population. Improvements in living standards would also result from the governmental and societal changes that are required for economic reform. Citizens and firms alike would gain from the state's growing more responsive to the needs of society and allowing a free and rapid flow of information, both within the Soviet Union and across its borders.

By imparting vigor to the Soviet system, reformers plan to create a more attractive model for other countries to emulate, thereby enhancing Soviet prestige and authority in the global arena. The USSR's world standing, they believe, is determined above all by its ability to contribute to the international system and the resolution of problems common to humankind. Military might remains an important means of wielding power but only insofar as it complements, rather than replaces, internal dynamism.

Gorbachev and his supporters have reshaped Soviet foreign policy to push forward the process of domestic reform. In the immediate term, they have directed their endeavors toward alleviating Western pressure. Overcoming enmity and instability in the international environment is crucial for carrying out internal reconstruction that is far more contentious, disruptive, and costly than a simple shift in resources from the military to the civilian sector. The establishment of cooperative East-West relations over the long run offers the USSR the opportunity to join the international system. The Soviet Union, in Gorbachev's view, cannot master modern technology in isolation from other countries. The USSR must learn from Western experience by granting Soviet citizens access to Western ideas, fostering interaction between Soviet and foreign institutions, and placing the Soviet economy in direct competition with the most industrially advanced nations. The Soviet Union can produce goods and provide services approaching world standards only by participating fully in the international community and global economy.

Soviet security policy advances the prospects for *perestroika* by enhancing military and political stability. The Brezhnev Politburo accepted nuclear parity and mutual deterrence and eschewed confrontation. The USSR under Gorbachev attaches much greater value to stability, granting precedence to stability over the accumulation of military power and striving to remove the sources of conflict with the United States and Western Europe. A durable balance of military and political interests constitutes an essential precondition for expanding East-West cooperation and for restructuring Soviet defenses. It creates an environment, at home and abroad, that is conducive to the downgrading of military priorities and to reform of the armed forces.

Gorbachev inherited a bloated military establishment that hindered improved relations with the West and encumbered industrial modernization. He was therefore determined to reduce the defense burden to a level that the Soviet economy could sustain while undergoing a transition from central planning to a mixed market. Moreover, members of the political leadership and of the high command recognized the pressing need to revitalize the technological base of the economy with the help of inputs from the defense industry in order to strengthen the technological competitiveness of Soviet weaponry. The creation of modern armed forces cannot be achieved by concentrating technological resources in the defense sector but instead requires the production of advanced technology in all major areas of industry. By rendering military capabilities commensurate with the economic and technological potential of the Soviet Union, the Gorbachev leadership ensures that Soviet military might presents both an affordable and effective means to exert influence.

Soviet policy on nuclear disarmament is designed to provide external and internal conditions that promote the modernization of the Soviet system. Arms reduction serves to relieve the USSR of Western pressure. In 1985, Gorbachev and his supporters focused attention on disarmament as the most readily available way to temper the threat from the United States. Arms control was a familiar instrument of diplomacy that had formed the principal topic of dialogue between the superpowers. However, as a means for substantially improving superpower relations, arms control on its own was clearly insufficient. The USSR had to alter its behavior throughout the international arena, particularly in the Third World, and to carry out domestic reform in order to convince the West to engage in genuine cooperation. Thus buttressed by wide-ranging changes in Soviet foreign policy, reductions in nuclear weapons decreased Western hostility, reinforced common interests with the West, removed obstacles to Soviet involvement in the world system, and thereby provided the USSR with entry into the international community.

The strengthening of international stability and development of constructive interaction with the West undermined political forces in Moscow that supported the continued buildup of Soviet military capabilities. Nuclear disarmament constrained the exercise of military power overseas and diminished the claim of the armed forces on resources, thus facilitating the realignment of Soviet military might with the country's economic and technological potential. Industrial capacity and technological resources released from the defense sector are being transferred to the civilian economy. Furthermore, arms reduction bolsters efforts to boost the productivity of military plants and to reconfigure Soviet forces. It eases the pressure to sustain high levels of weapons procurement during the disruptive process of restructuring the defense complex, and it provides the predictability required for planning the development and production of modern armaments. Since military power is primarily a function of the sophistication of personnel and weaponry, according to advocates of military reform, and smaller armed forces can be better trained and equipped, cuts in the size of nuclear arsenals furnish savings that can be spent on procuring technologically advanced weapon systems.

The book is divided into six chapters. The first five explore, respectively, the domestic political, economic, security, military, and diplomatic components of Soviet arms control policy. Chapter 6 draws on the preceding analysis to interpret Soviet aims and priorities in disarmament negotiations.

Chapter 1 examines the personnel and institutional changes that gave impetus to revisions in Soviet security policy. Gorbachev and his supporters assigned high priority to improved East-West relations and to nuclear disarmament as means for stimulating the Soviet system's modernization. By removing conservatives from the leadership and shifting political authority from the Communist Party to the Supreme Soviet, they bolstered support for the reform process and for "new political thinking." They curtailed the military's influence and filled the high command with modernists who were prepared to raise the quality of the Soviet armed forces with fewer resources and to modify Soviet strategy to enhance stability. The Gorbachev leadership consolidated civilian expertise on arms control to reassess Soviet force requirements and to identify political benefits that could be derived from relinquishing particular Soviet military advantages.

The second chapter explores the strong economic inducements for the Soviet Union to pursue disarmament. The reform program has raised consumer expectations but failed to spur Soviet economic growth, so the Gorbachev leadership has instructed the defense complex to increase output of consumer goods and to supply civilian industry with the advanced technology needed to improve productivity. Over time, arms reductions promise to contribute significantly to economic modernization as industrial and scientific potential is released from the military sector and converted to civilian uses. Disarmament also generates stable international conditions for restructuring the defense complex to produce sophisticated new weapons at an affordable cost.

Changes in Soviet national security aims, investigated in Chapter 3, provide the rationale for undertaking nuclear disarmament. New political thinking downgrades military force as a source of Soviet power and recognizes that the external threat is partly of Soviet making, so it prescribes greater reliance on diplomacy and less on military might to protect Soviet interests. Limiting the Soviet arms buildup and offering other large concessions to alleviate Western concerns encourages restraint on the part of the West and fosters more stable and cooperative relations. New thinking drives the USSR to compromise with the West to achieve substantial arms reductions.

Chapter 4 analyzes the impact of revisions in nuclear strategy on force requirements and on Soviet disarmament initiatives. The adoption of a no-first-use doctrine raised the importance of enhancing military stability and developing the capacity to wage war employing only conventional weapons. These changes in strategy confirmed Soviet opposition to ballistic missile defenses, stimulated substantial cuts in, and reconfiguration of, the Soviet strategic arsenal, and generated momentum toward ridding Europe of nuclear arms. Prominent civilian strategists advocate a shift to minimum deterrence but face resistance from the military leadership, which intends to retain some elements of a nuclear war-fighting capability.

Soviet pursuit of foreign policy objectives through arms control is appraised in Chapter 5. Putting new thinking into practice, the USSR promotes an overall improvement in the East-West climate by wielding less military power and expanding its involvement with the West. Nuclear disarmament serves to stabilize the superpowers' military relationship and the security structures of Europe. Large concessions from the Soviet Union appeal to moderates in the U.S. government to scale back American weapon programs, such as the Strategic Defense Initiative (SDI), and to deal constructively with the USSR. Soviet arms cuts are designed to reduce West European reliance on U.S. security commitments, to stifle movement toward military integration, and to stimulate the creation of a new European security system.

The final chapter interprets Soviet conduct of nuclear arms talks in light of the foregoing analysis of Soviet security, nuclear strategy, and foreign policy. The Soviet Union is scrapping intermediate- and short-range missiles and is pressing for reduction of tactical nuclear weapons in order to create a safe environment in Europe conducive to wide-scale cooperation. The Strategic Arms Reduction Treaty (START) substantially cuts strategic arms, placing ceilings on warheads and reducing land-based ballistic missiles in favor of aviation. It allows weapon modernization programs to continue but increases strategic stability and raises the prospects for further cuts leading to the eventual adoption of minimum deterrence. Soviet concessions permitting research into space-based defenses represent an effort to court lukewarm American supporters of SDI and make an offense-defense trade-off more attractive.

The book analyzes Soviet nuclear arms control policy from the accession of Gorbachev in March 1985 to the June 1990 agreement in principle to conclude a Strategic Arms Reduction Treaty. It draws on Soviet experience of the Brezhnev period and the first half of the 1980s as a point of reference, and projects trends in Soviet policy into the future. It is organized thematically rather than chronologically, but shows how Soviet behavior evolved over the course of Gorbachev's tenure.

The study makes no claim to offer a comprehensive documentation of the USSR's approach to nuclear disarmament. Instead, it concentrates on interpreting the major decisions affecting nuclear weapons in Europe, strategic arms, and ballistic missile defenses. It devotes scant attention to events of little consequence, examines selective aspects of questions related to the central focus—for example, conventional arms reductions and the East European dimension of nuclear weapons cuts—and leaves out important issues such as verification, nuclear testing, non-proliferation, and Chinese nuclear forces. The breadth of the subject matter prevents certain topics from being explored in great depth. In particular, the book fails to do justice to the variety of Soviet opinions. The coherence of the argument is maintained by presenting only those Soviet views that best explain change, and continuity, in Soviet behavior.

Since the book relies heavily on Soviet sources, their use deserves explanation. Soviet speeches and writings are obviously helpful in interpreting Soviet actions, because the sweeping reassessment of declared Soviet interests was accompanied by fundamental shifts in Soviet disarmament policy and because specific changes in Soviet views are consistent with particular decisions and trends in the USSR's conduct of arms talks. A large part of the Soviet debate addresses general questions such as the utility of military might and the benefits of compromising with the West. Though couched at times in lofty rhetoric, views on broad issues shape specific positions, on force requirements or security arrangements, for instance, that have a direct bearing on arms control. Thus, shifts in Soviet opinion elucidate the reasons for change in the Soviet stance on nuclear disarmament. Disagreements and affirmations of new beliefs reflect controversy over, and modifications in, Soviet aims. Although justifications and appeals for action might obscure the speaker's motives, Soviet pronouncements constitute substantive political discourse.

The study focuses on new thinking to expose the sources of revisions in Soviet policy. Opposing viewpoints are presented to show why change is hindered. The debate appearing in the Soviet media and specialized literature is lopsided. Arguments consonant with new thinking tend to receive more exposure in public than private because they advocate change and form the views in political ascendancy. Proponents of new thinking reassess past Soviet experience, question old assumptions, revise Soviet objectives, and lay out options for decision makers. They enjoy the backing of the most powerful men in Moscow. They espouse a cause that is difficult to contradict in public. Individuals who gain a reputation for criticizing new thinking can expect their political influence to wane.

Challenging the new thinking is less urgent than promoting it. Conservatives do not set out to change minds. They seek to preserve existing policy and to impede modifications in Soviet behavior. If traditional thinkers lose the debate, they can stifle implementation of change, so instead of attacking new thinking head on, they tend to endorse its general premises while blocking specific policy shifts. They often argue in oblique ways, at times by proxy, or respond to demands for change with public silence.

The political strength of every Soviet official is limited to some degree. The president is by far the most powerful leader in the USSR, and his remarks carry more weight than those of anyone else, but he must still persuade skeptics and convert audiences to his position. His statements reflect policy only insofar as they receive the endorsement of key political players and are translated into action. The president, defense minister, and others spend much time exhorting recalcitrant subordinates to carry out declared policy and to put reforms promptly and fully into practice.

Much of the public discourse of interest to this study takes place at the lower echelons of government. The arguments of Supreme Soviet deputies, Communist Party officials, diplomats, military officers, and natural and social scientists are in themselves of relatively little consequence but deserve close scrutiny. Any one of these individuals finds himself among many peers of equal political standing. His views are noteworthy if they become the prevailing opinion in Moscow or gain the assent of decision makers. Experts prepare detailed assessments of world developments, broach new topics for consideration, and devise ways to achieve Soviet objectives. They sometimes urge the leadership to reconsider its position on a given issue. On other occasions they are called upon to elaborate the specifics of policy, particularly when it is promulgated in broad and ambiguous terms. Gorbachev has introduced some new concepts, such as the "common European home," to invite discussion on what constitutes the Soviet aim and how to attain it. Therefore, the debate among experts sheds a great deal of light on the motives for change in Soviet policy.

1

INNOVATION IN POLICY FORMATION

The Gorbachev leadership's ascent to power paved the way for the transformation of Soviet nuclear arms control policy. Gorbachev and his supporters were by instinct reformers committed to revitalizing the Soviet system. They took personal charge of foreign policy and disarmament issues to ensure that rapid progress was achieved in these areas and that, as a result, resources were redirected from the defense sector to the civilian economy. They weakened resistance to "new political thinking" by weeding conservatives out of the top echelons of the government and the Communist Party and by molding institutions to render them more responsive to the needs of reform.

Officials in the highest military posts were replaced by commanders willing to accept increasingly tight constraints on the defense budget and to restructure the armed forces to enhance their technological competitiveness at lower cost. The military's influence in decision-making bodies waned as institutional checks on the armed forces were strengthened and civilian input into the formulation of arms control policy grew. The Supreme Soviet, exercising its authority as a reconstituted legislature, placed the high command's assessment of Soviet defense requirements under detailed scrutiny. Gorbachev and his associates enlisted the support of diplomats and academics to encroach on areas of policymaking previously reserved for the General Staff. They assembled staffs of civilian experts on military affairs and augmented ties to research institutes to promote changes in nuclear strategy, to devise alternative force postures, to indicate which military advantages could be traded for political benefits, and to craft Soviet initiatives on disarmament.

MANEUVERING IN THE LEADERSHIP

Gorbachev entered the office of General Secretary in March 1985 committed to reform. His speeches exposed many of the problems pervading the Soviet economy and stressed the need to improve relations with the West.[1] He has articulated a vision, which has grown more radical over time, of the system that he seeks to create.[2] His domestic program has proved erratic because, as Gorbachev himself admits, mistakes were made,[3] but his foreign policy has evolved with consistency as he consolidated his leadership and gained the confidence of Western governments. Though he reportedly devotes many hours to devising policy strategies with his advisors, Gorbachev is regarded most highly as a masterful tactician. He has pushed reform, setting the agenda and launching initiatives, but has held the middle ground in order to contain the criticism of Stalinist conservatives. Gorbachev has demonstrated political acumen, taking full advantage of promising opportunities and, when he encountered stiff opposition, waiting for a more propitious moment to advance. He has engineered changes in the Soviet leadership and encouraged purges of party and government bureaucracies in order to surmount resistance to his program.

Gorbachev has assigned top priority to reshaping Soviet security policy. Upon his accession, he embarked on a review of military strategy[4] and indicated his wish to cut defense spending. Gorbachev took personal charge of foreign relations and conducted a growing number of diplomatic meetings. He replaced Andrei Gromyko as foreign minister in July 1985 with Eduard Shevardnadze. The selection came as a surprise even to Shevardnadze himself, but Gorbachev's insistence overcame Shevardnadze's misgivings about accepting the job offer.[5]

Shevardnadze had built a reputation for fighting corruption and encouraging reform experiments in his native Georgian republic. He distinguished himself as an open-minded leader and as the only identifiable supporter of Gorbachev in the Politburo. Shevardnadze had gained some exposure to international issues and formed strong opinions of his own.[6] His experience of domestic problems gave him a deep understanding of the internal restructuring that Gorbachev's foreign policy was meant to promote.

The other member of the leadership most closely associated to Gorbachev, Aleksandr Yakovlev, acquired greater responsibilities for international affairs. Yakovlev was elevated in 1985 from director of the Academy of Sciences' Institute of World Economy and International Relations (known by its Russian acronym *IMEMO*) to head of the Central Committee's Propaganda Department. He entered the Secretariat in March 1986 to oversee ideology and foreign policy. He joined the Politburo as a candidate member in January 1987 and rose to full membership in June. Throughout his rapid ascent in the leadership, Yakovlev advised Gorbachev on foreign relations, accompanied him on most important diplomatic missions, and elaborated new thinking.

The Politburo established a commission to examine the military aspects of Soviet foreign policy and to prepare the Soviet position at the arms talks.[7] The commission functioned as a Politburo subcommittee that drafted documents collectively and assigned responsibility to individual members to implement its directives. It focused the leadership's attention on the military component of Soviet security and dealt with disarmament as a high priority. It provided an alternative to the Defense Council and cut some of the Politburo's conservatives out of decision making.

Improvement in relations with the West and progress in arms control have, in Gorbachev's view, been crucial for undertaking internal reform.[8] They have weakened the high command's claim on resources and stimulated military reform.[9] They have directed the leadership to examine weapon programs more critically and have warranted greater input of civilian experts in formulating defense policy. Disarmament, in developing a legal framework to regulate competition in nuclear arms, also reinforces efforts to establish a law-governed Soviet state.

Relaxation of world tensions reduces the dangers of domestic restructuring. The repercussions of reform—growing discontent among workers and bureaucrats, intensifying political polarization, and increasing nationalist unrest—generate a great risk of instability. In a friendly international environment, the Gorbachev leadership could loosen its grip on Soviet society and withstand the strains in the USSR's political fabric that resulted from *perestroika*. The opening to the West advanced "democratization" at home[10] and raised the possibility of attaining Western assistance.

By setting foreign affairs at the top of their agenda and replacing key decision makers, Gorbachev and his supporters managed to put new thinking into practice. Since fewer people were required for its implementation, Soviet foreign policy was much easier to change than domestic policy. While *perestroika* remains an arduous process that has yet to yield material benefits, Gorbachev has provided tangible results of his leadership in the international sphere. In less than three years, he brought home a treaty that lowered, for the first time in history, the level of nuclear arms and removed entirely from Europe a threatening category of U.S. weapons. Success in foreign policy and arms control has enhanced Gorbachev's prestige and the authority of his leadership. When he comes under attack, he reminds his critics of his achievements in foreign relations and disarmament.[11]

Gorbachev faced opposition from Gromyko, Volodymyr Shcherbytsky, Yegor Ligachev, and Viktor Chebrikov, who expressed varying degrees of skepticism about the wisdom of making concessions on arms control and reaching agreements with the United States.[12] They obstructed change in Soviet policy from their seats on the Politburo. Chebrikov, as KGB chairman, also participated in the decision making of restricted leadership bodies (in the Defense Council and Politburo commission on political-military affairs).

Change in the leadership's composition was the precursor to policy innovation. From 1985, the Soviet Union followed a pattern of making large compromises or launching substantive initiatives on arms control in a space of two months after the demotion or retirement of powerful conservatives. Gromyko relinquished his post as foreign minister and assumed what was then the largely ceremonial position of chairman of the Presidium of the USSR Supreme Soviet (head of state) before the Soviet Union presented a new proposal on START (Strategic Arms Reduction Talks). The dismissal of Sergei Sokolov and promotion of Dmitri Yazov to defense minister laid the groundwork for Gorbachev to put forward the "double zero option," the plan to eliminate all short-range as well as intermediate-range nuclear missiles in Europe. The Central Committee plenum of September 1988—during which Gromyko left the Politburo, Ligachev was demoted from *de facto* second secretary of the Party and Chebrikov was replaced as head of the KGB—set the stage for significant unilateral reductions in Soviet conventional forces. A year later, Chebrikov's departure from the Politburo and Secretariat and Shcherbytsky's ouster from both the Politburo and the post of Ukrainian Party first secretary, which he had held since Brezhnev's rule, were followed by Soviet agreement to proceed with strategic arms cuts in the absence of an explicit link to the Anti-Ballistic Missile Treaty. Finally, once the Politburo's authority had been sharply curtailed and Ligachev had retired at the 28th Party Congress in July 1990, the USSR was prepared to accept the inclusion of a unified Germany in the NATO alliance.

Gorbachev's sizable personal authority notwithstanding, the Politburo remained a collective leadership. A general consensus was required to alter the direction of policy. Gorbachev encountered resistance along the way, which constrained the scope and pace of change. Through skillful maneuvering, he brought dedicated reformers into the leadership and shifted the balance in favor of policy innovation. As the standing of the reform element increased, policy change grew more profound. Changes in the leadership fostered personnel turnover in party and government agencies and thereby dampened the influence of entrenched bureaucratic interests.

The shift of state power from the Communist Party to the Supreme Soviet bolstered the reform forces. Much of the party sought to protect the established position of its members and to hinder restructuring. The competitively elected Congress of People's Deputies, which in turn elected the Supreme Soviet, ensured that the legislature was more responsive to popular demands. Converted from a rubber stamp into a functioning legislature, the Supreme Soviet could help to elaborate the reform program and to oversee its implementation.

An early indication of the diminishing party say over foreign policy was the political rank of Anatoli Dobrynin, who ran the Central Committee International Department from June 1986 to September 1988. Whereas his predecessor, Boris Ponomarev, held alternate membership in the Politburo, Dobrynin was denied a seat on that body. However, in contrast to Ponomarev, who concerned himself mostly with foreign communists and left-of-center parties and who limited his contacts with Westerners to opposition leaders, Dobrynin was given responsibility for East-West relations and arms control.

In the autumn of 1988, the Central Committee underwent a major reorganization. Dobrynin left to join Gorbachev's newly assembled personal staff. The International Department, which merged with the Socialist Countries Department, was placed under the authority of a new Central Committee Commission on International Policy, chaired by Yakovlev. The Commission has met infrequently and has taken care not to interfere with the work of the Foreign Ministry.[13] The Central Committee apparatus was cut substantially, and the party Secretariat began to meet sporadically.[14]

The Central Committee was weakened by Gorbachev's creation of a personal staff. The International Department had channeled reports from the government agencies and prepared briefing papers for the General Secretary. With his own advisors,

Gorbachev relies much less on the Central Committee for information and policy analysis.

During the spring and summer of 1990, the functions of the party and the government were separated. Government leaders were made accountable solely to the Supreme Soviet and the state president. At the 28th Party Congress in July, they all resigned from the Politburo, and the Politburo was relegated to dealing only with party affairs. Thus, the party was left with little input into national policy and was prevented from meddling in the government's business.

Gorbachev retained control of the party and, at the 28th Congress, reaffirmed the principle of democratic centralism to impose party discipline on conservatives. He had consolidated his leadership in March 1990 by instituting an executive presidency. In addition to gaining some powers of decree and further centralizing state authority in his hands, Gorbachev freed himself of collective leadership. Top government officials have formed the Presidential Council, which is an advisory rather than executive body.[15]

CURTAILING THE MILITARY'S INFLUENCE

Gorbachev and his associates coopted the military leadership into implementing reform of Soviet defense policy. They reduced the political influence of the Defense Ministry, filled the high command with modernists who generally approved of *perestroika*, and exercised tight control over the armed forces. They thereby succeeded in pressuring the military into going along with large cuts in nuclear arsenals.

The political standing of the armed forces declined under Gorbachev. Brezhnev's defense minister, Dmitri Ustinov, had held full membership in the Politburo, but Sokolov and Yazov were merely candidate members. From 1985, the defense minister lacked voting rights in the Soviet Union's highest decision-making body. The contrast with the foreign minister and the head of the KGB, who were full Politburo members, reflected the political weakness of the military relative to that of the diplomatic and intelligence establishments. The ministers and KGB chairman presently enjoy equal status in the Presidential Council, but only as advisors.

Gorbachev used his power of appointment to constrain the military's influence. Bypassing the normal hierarchies, he selected relatively junior people who would, at least initially, be beholden to him, and he brought in officers from outside of military institutions who would show greater enthusiasm for reforming them. Army General Yuri Maksimov, appointed chief of the Strategic Missile Forces in July 1985, came from the ground services. He accepted reductions in the size and prestige of land-based nuclear forces. Marshal Yazov was an Army general serving as deputy defense minister for personnel in May 1987 when he was elevated to the post of defense minister. Yazov was pulled up from below more senior officers because he had distinguished himself early on as a supporter of *perestroika*.[16] The promotion of Mikhail Moiseyev to chief of the General Staff in December 1988 was highly unusual. He was not only quite junior but also an outsider, having never been assigned previously to the General Staff.

Moiseyev succeeded Marshal Sergei Akhromeyev, who resigned to become a personal advisor to Gorbachev. Akhromeyev had long been active in elaborating the high command's position on disarmament as well as in devising military strategy and force structures. At the Reykjavik and December 1987 Washington summits he led the Soviet side of the working group on arms control. In his present capacity, Akhromeyev devotes more attention to disarmament issues.[17]

The leadership of the armed forces is composed predominantly of modernists who seek to ensure the effectiveness of Soviet defense by developing technologically advanced weapon systems at an affordable cost. They recognize the dangers of nuclear war and the need to enhance strategic stability. They regard economic strength as an essential source of military power and tolerate some constraints on defense spending to pay for the reconstruction of the USSR's industrial base. In the view of the modernists, large quantities of armaments provide an inadequate substitute for their poor quality, because the Soviet Union's combat potential rests primarily on the technological sophistication of its weaponry.

Military modernists favor the lowering of arms levels and restructuring of the armed forces and the defense industry. They disagree with political authorities on the size of arms cuts and reductions in defense expenditure and resist interference by the political leadership and civilian experts in determining military strategy and force structures, but they concur with Gorbachev's efforts to modify Soviet defense policy. They endorsed the broad concept of military sufficiency and, in 1988, the construction of defenses along qualitative parameters. The high command is now heavily involved in carrying out military reform. Army General Moiseyev is running a commission that is drawing up a long-term plan to restructure the armed services.[18]

The political leadership applied strong pressure on the high command to assist in formulating proposals for arms reduction. The military aspects of foreign policy were examined by the special Politburo commission and by the Defense Council, which was composed of many of the same members as the Politburo commission but with greater input from military officers and industrialists. The Defense Council, whose role has been assumed by the Presidential Council,[19] tackled arms control questions, evaluating the consequences of disarmament measures, for example.[20] Decisions were made collectively, as government leaders emphasized at the 28th Party Congress. In the special Politburo commission, Zaikov disclosed, if one member raised an objection to a policy document, it was sent back to the staff for additional revision.[21]

The military leadership endorsed all Soviet arms control initiatives, but at times did so grudgingly. Akhromeyev stressed that the exclusion of British and French forces from the INF talks was a political, not military, decision that the General Staff had difficultly accepting.[22] In the case of the unilateral reductions in conventional forces announced by Gorbachev at the United

Nations in December 1988, the Politburo had instructed the high command to come up with a substantial figure for troop and tank cuts.[23] The political leadership has exercised strict control over Soviet military policy, and the platform of the 28th Congress reaffirmed the leadership's determination to preserve firm political authority in the defense sphere.[24]

CIVILIANS MASTER DEFENSE POLICY

Gorbachev transformed the decision-making process from the secretive deliberations confined to the very top leadership of the early 1980s to more open debate among all interested political groups. At the 19th Conference of the Communist Party of the Soviet Union, he criticized the "command-administrative methods" employed in the past formulation of foreign policy, noting that even the most important decisions used to be made by a narrow circle of individuals. Under Gorbachev, Soviet policy options have been widely discussed. The Soviet stance on disarmament was devised by the working group of the special Politburo commission, which was composed of experts from the Foreign and Defense Ministries, the Military-Industrial Commission, the KGB, the Central Committee, and the Academy of Sciences.[25]

Participation in the formulation of Soviet arms control policy has expanded, primarily at the expense of the military. Nongovernmental actors, such as natural and social scientists, have become heavily involved. The Supreme Soviet joined the policy debate. Institutions traditionally responsible for Soviet security policy increased their input into decision making by upgrading their sectors dealing with arms control and strengthening their ties to the research institutes of the Academy of Sciences.

Shevardnadze cleaned out the upper ranks of the Foreign Ministry, getting rid of Gromyko's first deputies and seven of his eight deputy ministers.[26] The exception, Anatoli Kovalev, a specialist on European affairs whose career had stalled during the early 1980s, was promoted to first deputy foreign minister. The personnel changes elevated experienced diplomats sympathetic to new thinking who had the inclination and now the license to explore new ideas and make serious efforts to resolve diplomatic disputes.

The Foreign Ministry augmented its authority on arms control in 1986 by bringing together various sectors into a Directorate of Arms Limitation and Disarmament. The directorate was put under the charge of veteran arms negotiator Viktor Karpov, who in November 1988 was named deputy foreign minister. In January 1987, the chief delegates to the Nuclear and Space Talks (NST) were raised, at Soviet suggestion, to the level of first deputy foreign minister, and the job was filled by Yuli Vorontsov.[27]

Since Shevardnadze attaches great value to the views of scholars, the Ministry reinforced its links to outside experts. It created a Scientific Information Center to coordinate academic research. Most departments of the Foreign Ministry established consultative councils to let scholars voice their opinions on international issues.[28] The councils are designed to improve communication with research analysts and to facilitate the incorporation of new ideas into Soviet foreign policy.

Shortly after taking charge of the International Department of the Central Committee, Dobrynin set up a department of military affairs and disarmament. Its director was Lt. Gen. Viktor Starodubov, a high-ranking expert on arms control. In late 1988, Gorbachev assembled a staff of personal advisors on national security that included Dobrynin, Starodubov (who is currently assigned to the General Staff), and Akhromeyev. The staff reduces Gorbachev's reliance on the military for assessments of policy options.

The reconstituted Supreme Soviet began in late 1989 to gain some authority over security policy. It oversees government operations, confirms ministers, and approves the state budget. It has a large say on such paramount issues as spending levels, military procurement, and use of military forces overseas. Much of its substantive work is conducted in the Joint Committees on International Affairs and on Defense and State Security. The International Affairs Committee has heard testimony on nuclear test bans and foreign economic relations and has monitored Soviet compliance with the January 1989 Vienna accords on human rights.

Reformers have criticized the Defense Committee's lack of independence. It has a staff of only ten people, holds most of its hearings in closed sessions, and is filled almost entirely with people professionally connected in some way to the armed forces or the defense complex.[29] Nevertheless, the committee has carried out significant work, soliciting views from government officials and outside experts; examining details of the defense budget; overseeing the armed services, including the Strategic Missile Forces; making recommendations on weapons production; analyzing problems of industrial conversion; and even taking legislative initiatives, for instance, drafting a proposal to establish a professional army.[30]

Enhancing the authority of the Supreme Soviet helps to curtail the military's influence. The national legislature subjects the plans of the armed forces to detailed scrutiny. It widens participation in policy deliberation and decision making, involving also Supreme Soviet deputies without much expertise on security matters. The legislature strengthens the exercise of civilian control over the high command and thereby induces greater moderation in Soviet defense policy.

The Academy of Sciences has assumed a prominent role in assisting the formulation of Gorbachev's policy. Members of the research institutes participate in interagency committees, most notably in the working group of the Politburo commission on political-military affairs, that assess the international situation and draw up policy options for the leadership's consideration. They enjoy firm links to the government and regular access to decision makers, and thus have ample opportunities to broach ideas. Some scientists have gone on to serve in high party and government positions.

Yevgeni Primakov, former head of *IMEMO*, joined the Central Committee Commission on International Policy. He was elected candidate Politburo member in September 1989 and served as chairman of the Supreme Soviet Council of the Union, one of the two legislative chambers, until March 1990. He resigned from the Politburo in July to devote full time to his duties on the Presidential Council.

Yevgeni Velikhov, vice president of the Academy of Sciences and chairman of the Committee of Soviet Scientists for Peace, has long been active in conducting substantive research with important policy implications and preparing reports on disarmament. He enjoyed a high standing in the party as part of the Central Committee Commission on International Policy and now leads the Armed Forces Subcommittee of the Supreme Soviet Defense Committee.

Director of the USA Institute Georgi Arbatov also served on the Central Committee Commission and has been placed in charge of the Supreme Soviet International Affairs Subcommittee on Foreign Policy and Legal Questions. Arbatov wanted the legislature to exercise greater supervisory powers over arms control and to oversee the entire course of negotiations rather than evaluate each disarmament agreement only after it had been signed and required ratification.[31] In March 1990, the Supreme Soviet Committees on Defense and International Affairs discussed the Nuclear and Space Talks and the negotiations on Conventional Forces in Europe (CFE).[32]

Recommendations from natural and social scientists have been incorporated in Soviet security policy. The high command threatened to respond to Reagan's Strategic Defense Initiative (SDI) with its own antiballistic missiles until a study by the Committee of Soviet Scientists for Peace showed that offensive countermeasures are much cheaper. After the results of the study were disseminated, Soviet generals vowed to beef up Soviet offensive capabilities if the United States deployed strategic defenses, and the arms negotiators tied a deal on START to restraints on SDI development. The plan of Vitali Zhurkin, director of the Institute of Europe, for building a common European home provided the basis for Shevardnadze's proposals. Zhurkin advocated a gradual replacement of the military blocs by a collective security system:

arms reductions would erode the military command structures, and the increasingly political alliances would develop contacts and consultations that would grow into permanent ties and pan-European institutions.[33] Some months later, Shevardnadze called for further measures to surmount the military confrontation on the continent and for cooperation between the North Atlantic Treaty Organization (NATO) and the Warsaw Pact, including annual summit meetings of the Conference on Security and Cooperation in Europe (CSCE), the creation of a CSCE Foreign Ministers Committee, and the establishment of multilateral agencies of CSCE.[34]

During Gorbachev's tenure, civilian agencies began seriously to vie with the armed services as sources of expertise on technical military matters. Through twenty years of experience in studying arms control and Western defense policies, members of the research institutes and officials of the Foreign Ministry and the Central Committee apparatus had mastered such arcane subjects as nuclear strategy and force postures. Furthermore, these agencies took on retired or seconded military officers who tended to share the outlook of their civilian colleagues.

Gorbachev and his associates enlisted the support of civilian experts to inject greater political content into Soviet security policy. Dobrynin and Yakovlev instructed scholars to conduct research on the interrelationship between offensive and defensive, and between nuclear and conventional, weapons, on arms limitation and disarmament, and on reasonable sufficiency.[35] This research encroaches on areas previously reserved for analysis only by the military.

The General Staff had traditionally elaborated doctrinal concepts into military strategy and provided the information and analysis needed by the Defense Council and Politburo to set defense policy.[36] Civilian specialists had for some time competed with the General Staff in evaluating political-military conditions in the world. Under Gorbachev, they began to assess Soviet military strategy and weapon systems, which had been the prerogative of the armed services. Top military officers resent the intrusion and charge civilian experts with a lack of competence on military affairs.[37] The civilians, in turn, complain that they are denied access to important military data.[38]

Civilian strategists have broken the virtual monopoly of the armed forces on technical military expertise and have thereby relieved the political leadership of its heavy dependence on the high command for advice and policy options. They have used their newly acquired institutional authority to challenge the General Staff's assessments of force requirements, to identify Soviet military advantages that can be traded for political gains, and to craft constructive arms control proposals. Thus, civilians provide the expertise for the Gorbachev leadership to maintain the initiative and to forge progress in nuclear disarmament.

The changes introduced by Gorbachev in the Soviet leadership and the security policy-making establishment determined both the direction and content of Soviet nuclear arms control policy. By attaching fundamental importance to foreign affairs and disarmament; promoting reform-minded generals, diplomats, and political leaders; and reshaping institutions to meet his needs, Gorbachev managed to alter radically the Soviet approach to arms control. He formed a broad consensus in favor of redefining the USSR's defense requirements, cutting military spending, transferring a substantial amount of resources to the civilian sector, and restructuring the defense complex. He garnered enough political backing to reduce the military component of Soviet foreign policy, to pursue accommodation with the West, and to move toward Soviet integration into the international community.

The substance of Soviet policy on nuclear disarmament changed as a result of personnel turnover at the upper-middle level of government, wider participation in decision making, the enhanced institutional clout of civilian arms control experts, and the instructions given to civilian strategists to reexamine Soviet nuclear strategy and force postures. The reformers, particularly the diplomats and academics, used their increased input into Soviet policy on disarmament to broach new ideas, to provide the leadership with a wider array of policy options, to propose ways of restructuring nuclear arsenals to strengthen military and political stability, and to devise arms control initiatives that corresponded closely to Gorbachev's broad policy objectives. Injecting greater political content into the details of Soviet arms control policy, they identified particular Soviet weapon systems whose elimination would yield large political dividends and determined which Western arms programs to allow so as to avoid raising Western suspicions and bringing the disarmament process to a standstill.

NOTES

1. *Pravda*, 19 December 1984, 21 February 1985 and 12 March 1985.
2. Mikhail S. Gorbachev, *Perestroika* (London: Collins, 1987); and interview in *Time*, 4 June 1990.
3. Gorbachev in *Time*, p. 32.
4. Sergei F. Akhromeyev, "Novaya Politika Protiv Arsenalov Voyny" ["A New Policy Against the Arsenals of War"], *Kommunist Vooruzhennykh Sil* [*Communist of the Armed Forces*], no. 1 (January), 1990, p. 17.
5. Interview in *Ogonek*, no. 11 (March), 1990, p. 3.
6. Ibid.
7. Shevardnadze in *Izvestia*, 22 March 1989, and Lev Zaikov speech to the 28th Party Congress, *Pravda*, 4 July 1990. The commission, headed by Zaikov, included Yakovlev, Shevardnadze, the defense minister, the KGB chairman, and leaders of the Military-Industrial Commission, the Council of Ministers, and other departments.
8. Speech to the 28th Party Congress, *Pravda*, 11 July 1990.
9. Dmitri Yazov in *Krasnaya Zvezda*, 5 June 1990.
10. Alex Pravda, "Linkages between Soviet Domestic and Foreign Policy under Gorbachev," in Tsuyoshi Hasegawa and Alex Pravda (eds.), *Perestroika: Soviet Domestic and Foreign Policies* (London: Royal Institute of International Affairs, 1990), p. 3.
11. *Pravda*, 11 July 1990.
12. Details in Bruce Parrott, "Soviet National Security Under Gorbachev," *Problems of Communism*, vol. 37, no. 6 November/December 1988.
13. Yakovlev in *Pravda*, 4 July 1990, and present commission chairman Gennadi I. Yanayev in *Pravda*, 13 August 1990.
14. Ligachev in *Pravda*, 5 July 1990.

15. Yakovlev and Interior Minister Vadim Bakatin interviewed in *Izvestia*, 7 April 1990.
16. Dale R. Herspring, "Gorbachev, Yazov, and the Military," *Problems of Communism*, July/August 1987, vol. 36, no. 4, pp. 104-5.
17. *Krasnaya Zvezda*, 2 July 1989.
18. *Krasnaya Zvezda*, 13 April 1990.
19. Gorbachev in *Pravda*, 17 March 1990.
20. Zaikov in *Pravda*, 4 July 1990.
21. Ibid.
22. *Sovetskaya Rossia*, 12 May 1990.
23. Sergei F. Akhromeyev, "Kakiye Vooruzhennye Sily Nuzhny Sovetskomu Soyuzu?" ["Which Armed Forces Does the Soviet Union Need?"] *Ogonek*, no. 50 (December), 1989, p. 6.
24. *Pravda*, 27 June 1990.
25. Zaikov in *Pravda*, 4 July 1990.
26. Jerry F. Hough, "Gorbachev Consolidating Power," *Problems of Communism*, July/August 1987, vol. 36, no. 4, p. 33.
27. *Pravda*, 14 January 1987.
28. Eduard Shevardnadze, "Diplomatia i Nauka: Soyuz vo Imya Budushchevo" ["Diplomacy and Science: An Alliance for the Future"], *Kommunist*, no. 2 (January), 1990, p. 18.
29. Georgi M. Sturua, "Komitet po Voprosam Oborony i Gosudarstvennoy Bezopasnosti: Pervye Mesyatsy Raboty" ["The Committee for Defense and State Security: The First Months of Work"], *Mirovaya Ekonomika i Mezhdunarodnye Otnoshenia (MEMO)* [World Economy and International Relations], January 1990, pp. 83-84.
30. Ibid., *Krasnaya Zvezda*, 6 April 1990, and *Izvestia*, 11 April 1990.
31. *Pravda*, 17 October 1988.
32. *Izvestia*, 7 March 1990.
33. *Pravda*, 17 May 1989.
34. *Pravda*, 20 December 1989, and *Izvestia*, 19 January 1990.
35. Anatoli Dobrynin, "Za Bezyaderny Mir, Navstrechu XXI Veku" ["For a Nuclear Free World, to Meet the 21st Century"], *Kommunist*, no. 9 (June), 1986, pp. 26-27, and Aleksandr Yakovlev, "Dostizheniye Kachestvenno Novovo Sostoyania Sovetskovo Obshchestva i Obshchestvenniye Nauki" ["The Achievement of a Qualitatively New State of Soviet Society and the Social Sciences"], *Kommunist*, no. 8 (May), 1987, p. 18.
36. Condoleezza Rice, "The Party, the Military, and Decision Authority in the Soviet Union," *World Politics*, vol. 40, no. 1 (October 1987), pp. 55, 65-66.
37. Akhromeyev in *Sovetskaya Rossia*, 12 May 1990, and Maj. Gen. German V. Kirilenko, "Zabota o Bezopasnosti ili . . . o Snizheny

Bezopasnosti?" *Kommunist Vooruzhennykh Sil* ["Concern about Security or the Reduction of Security?"], no. 11 (June), 1990, p. 42.

38. Georgi Arbatov, "Armia dlya Strany ili Strana dlya Army?" [An Army for the Country or a Country for the Army?], *Ogonek*, no. 5 (January), 1990, p. 4.

2

ECONOMIC INDUCEMENTS FOR DISARMAMENT

The Soviet leadership saw compelling economic reasons for engaging in disarmament. Arms reductions create the environment and provide the resources necessary to restructure the Soviet economy, including the defense complex. Since Gorbachev's industrial modernization program and reforms of economic management failed to arrest the decline in Soviet economic growth, he has relied increasingly on military industry to manufacture consumer goods and to supply advanced technology inputs to civilian machine building factories. Cuts in military expenditures, particularly in weapon procurements and in research and development, furnish industrial capacity and technological resources to modernize the USSR's industrial base, to boost productivity, and to stimulate economic growth.

Arms reductions can generate large savings over time. Conversion of defense industry to civilian uses requires initial investments and disrupts output in the immediate term, but it stimulates military reform, putting pressure on defense plants to increase their efficiency to produce higher-quality weapons while cutting costs. Substantial economic benefits can accrue over the long run if the Soviet leadership maintains its commitment to pursue restructuring and disarmament.

GROWTH AND REFORM

At the April 1985 Central Committee Plenum, one month after taking office, Gorbachev outlined a program of economic growth and reform, promising improvements in living conditions and industrial modernization. Reform of management, combined with a focused industrial strategy, was designed to accelerate economic output and thereby increase the availability and quality of housing, consumer goods, and health care.

The centerpiece of Gorbachev's policy was industrial modernization. Accelerated economic development would result from intensive growth, from more efficient utilization of available resources. Lower material intensiveness in manufacturing, higher returns on assets, and substantially increased labor productivity would be achieved by a complete overhaul of Soviet productive capacity. Industrial plants throughout the country would introduce technologically advanced equipment produced by the machine-building sector. So, an increased share of capital investments was directed toward retooling existing enterprises and accelerating the development of machine building.[1]

Machine building would provide the catalyst for industrial modernization and economic growth. The machine-building complex, boosting the volume and quality of its output, would generate technological improvements in all branches of manufacturing. It would furnish the equipment to retool factories, to automate lines of production, and thereby to raise labor productivity.[2] Increasing the quality of Soviet productive capacity would require advances in the level of technology, especially in critical areas. Within the machine-building sector, priority was assigned to machine tools, computers, instrument making, electrical equipment, and electronics. These branches were slated to grow far more rapidly than the sector as a whole.[3]

The leadership set ambitious output targets for the machine-building sector and closely monitored its performance. Plans for machine-building production were not fulfilled, and the leadership leveled heavy criticism at the sector's management. In fact, the plan was faulty. Machine-building factories, like those in all branches of the economy, were expected to retool and simultaneously to boost production. They were instructed to increase both the volume and quality of their output. The machine-building sector's performance did improve but failed to meet targets. During the first half of the 12th Five Year Plan (1986-91), the growth rate of machine-building output doubled but did not fulfill the plan. Ivan Silayev, who was then chairman of the Council of Ministers' Machine Building Bureau, ascribed the failure to meet output targets to supply problems and weaknesses in research and development, to "the initial imbalance between production plans and material and technical resources."[4] The problem of bottlenecked supplies, which had long existed, was exacerbated by the sharp rise in the planned rate of industrial renovation.[5]

Feeling strong pressure to increase dramatically the volume of its production, the machine-building sector sacrificed qualitative improvements. As a result, machine-building output incorporated meager technological advancements. In mid-1988, the emphasis was shifted from quantity to quality. Silayev announced a new machine-building strategy of concentrating on priority areas, primarily on research and development. Greater capital investments were channeled into research and experimental design work.[6] Government plans targeted inputs into electronics, automation and resource-saving equipment, and computers.[7]

The Soviet Union has grown progressively more involved in the global economy. The Gorbachev leadership initially pursued autarkic development, striving for technological self-sufficiency by attempting to apply the USSR's considerable scientific achievements to Soviet industry. After a year and a half in office, it realized that diffusion of technology in the Soviet economy required external competitive pressure. In January 1987, the USSR passed a law on joint ventures and granted to several Soviet ministries and enterprises the right to engage directly in foreign trade. Amendments in the law to permit virtually complete foreign control of joint ventures produced in 1989 a surge in the number of agreements signed.[8] The USSR worked toward membership in international economic organizations such as the World Bank and the International Monetary Fund, concluded investment treaties, and sought bilateral agreements on taxation. Shevardnadze expressed the hope that adoption of a law on property and of other legislation would render the Soviet Union more hospitable to overseas business.[9] Competition from Western firms is welcomed by officials of the State Foreign Economic Commission for affecting Soviet prices and rates of production and for weakening the monopolies of domestic suppliers.[10]

Reform of industry did more to disrupt than to enhance production. The Law on the State Enterprise, enacted in 1987, was designed to grant managers greater autonomy, to reduce bureaucratic meddling in their affairs, and to render firms financially accountable. Enterprise structures were reorganized to foster closer collaboration between research and development and production. Implementation of the law was marred by its inconsistencies. Industrial ministries were held responsible for meeting output targets, so they naturally continued to micro-manage plants under their jurisdiction. Furthermore, enterprises were expected to generate revenue from private sales by charging the distorted prices set by central planners. In the absence of market prices, profits offered a poor measure of an enterprise's efficiency.

As the program of industrial modernization was sagging, the rest of the Soviet economy was experiencing problems. Economic growth slowed to about 1.5 percent a year by 1987.[11] Growth in consumption was sluggish. Plans to boost economic output failed to be fulfilled, and promises for improved food supplies, consumer durables and housing were not met. The expectations that Gorbachev had raised remained frustrated.

The problem was compounded by inflation, both actual and hidden. The soaring state budget deficit and the wage reform, which allowed wages to grow faster than labor productivity, created an excess supply of money. This exacerbated shortages and raised prices of goods that were available. The financial imbalance convinced the leadership to put off price reform, which will be instrumental in establishing a properly functioning market of wholesale trade. Postponement of price reform has caused disruptions to persist in the implementation of changes in economic management.

By late 1987, the Gorbachev leadership began to alter course. Boosting consumption became the first priority. In October, Gorbachev acknowledged that the food problem was acute and enlisted the support of machine-building and military enterprises to satisfy the food industry's urgent needs.[12] At the 19th Party Conference in June 1988, Gorbachev identified poor food supplies as the most pressing problem facing the nation and expressed grave concern about shortages of housing and consumer goods. He instructed defense plants and heavy industry to increase "decisively" their contribution to the civilian sector.[13] In 1987, the growth rate of output of consumer goods began to surpass that of producer goods, and by the following year, capital investment in the social sphere was outpacing that in the productive sphere.[14]

Along with fulfilling expectations for higher living standards, normalizing economic conditions was designated a primary objective of the Gorbachev leadership. Manufacture of industrial goods continued to slow down as consumer goods production and housing construction accelerated. The state plan for 1990 intended to boost consumption and to achieve stabilization at the expense of economic growth. Regulation of money circulation and improvement in government finances would reduce distortions in the economy as output targets diminished.[15]

Concern to normalize the market situation caused hesitation on economic reform. By the summer of 1990, however, the Gorbachev leadership was set to embark on a transition to a regulated market economy. Gorbachev outlined his plan to the 28th Party Congress. He advocated a comprehensive approach to implementing economic restructuring. Enterprises would be removed from the control of government departments, and industrial branch ministries would eventually be abolished. The state would allow various forms of property and begin to privatize industry, leasing small firms, turning large state enterprises into joint stock companies, and establishing stock markets. The banking system would be revamped and price reform would be introduced. Henceforth, the government would pursue economic objectives, for instance, stimulate technological progress through taxes, interest rates, and other indirect means.[16]

With economic growth scheduled to remain slow, resources allocated increasingly to produce consumer goods, and a disappointing performance of the machine-building sector, the stalling program of industrial modernization threatened to grind to a halt unless the defense complex came to the rescue. The Gorbachev leadership, determined to keep industrial modernization on track, notwithstanding all other economic problems, decided to squeeze the defense sector. Substantial cuts in defense would help to boost output of consumer goods as well as provide resources for civilian machine building and plant retooling in all branches of industry.

EASING THE DEFENSE BURDEN

Defense spending was placing a severe strain on the Soviet economy when the modernization program was launched. Plans to invigorate Soviet industry were stifled by the large portion of machine-building output devoted to weapons production. Reduction in military procurement increased the availability of machinery for civilian uses and thereby contributed to improved economic performance.

The size of the defense burden on the Soviet economy is difficult to ascertain. The Soviet government provided no reliable data on its military expenditures until June 1989, when it offered a credible figure for total defense spending and some details on its defense budget. In the absence of useful Soviet statistics, Western observers have relied on their own estimates.

Of the different calculations of Soviet military expenditures, the most frequently cited is the Central Intelligence Agency's (CIA) "direct-costing" of defense outlays in rubles. The CIA measures Soviet military spending by adding up the ruble prices of various physical indicators: personnel costs, research, development, testing, engineering, operational costs, and weapons production. The ruble estimates are drawn initially from prevailing transaction prices. The initial estimates are then adjusted to factor-cost valuation. Subsidies are added and indirect taxes are subtracted to obtain prices that more closely reflect the cost of production. Where Soviet cost-estimate relationships are unavailable, particularly for most weapon systems, the costs are calculated in dollars and then converted into rubles. For example, if the ruble price of a ship were unobtainable, the CIA would calculate the cost of building that vessel in the United States and then convert the dollar price into rubles based on an estimate of the relative efficiency of Soviet and U.S. shipbuilding.

The CIA's figures have been challenged, by some for being too high, by others for being too low.[17] The CIA reaffirmed the reliability of the methods it uses to estimate Soviet defense spending[18] but left many critics unconvinced.[19] The size of the Soviet armed forces is not at issue. Rather, critics charge the CIA with miscalculating the cost of Soviet defense.

The CIA asserted that the Soviet defense burden grew from 14–16 percent of GNP in 1980 to 15–17 percent in 1988.[20] Since 1985, military outlays rose 3 percent a year in real terms while the annual rate of increase of Soviet GNP slowed down to about 1.5 percent.[21] The CIA ascribes the growth of the Soviet defense burden in the second half of the 1980s to a rise in prices. While the Soviet military did not become larger, it grew more costly because the price increases in the defense industry outpaced those in the civilian sector. Incorporation of more advanced technologies and modernization of the manufacturing base rendered new weapon systems far more expensive than their predecessors.[22] Gorbachev admits that military expenditure reached 18 percent of Soviet national income[23] and claims that Soviet defense spending was frozen in 1987 and 1988.[24]

The defense burden cannot be described by purely quantitative measurements. The large salaries paid to employees, the generous financing of research institutes, and the high quality of inputs, machinery and equipment in the defense sector are reflected in the ruble cost estimates of Soviet military spending. The figures fail to show that the best engineers, managers, and workers are found in defense industries. These employees enjoy special access to housing, medical care, and other amenities. Military factories are accorded top priority in claims for raw materials and inputs. Planning agencies deal more quickly with their requests, and when shortages or bottlenecks develop, supplies are redirected from civilian industries. Before *glasnost* reached the military sphere, the defense industry took full advantage of its secrecy to fend off rival claims for resources and criticism of its inefficiency in weapons production.

The defense sector, in contrast to the rest of the pre-reform economy, has traditionally been unique in allowing the consumer to play a powerful role. Military officers take part in weapons development and production. They are stationed at arms manufacturing plants to help overcome bottlenecks, to speed up the supply of inputs, and to ensure that production meets the high quality standards expected by the military. When faulty equipment is found, it is discarded or dumped in the civilian sector. The priority accorded to defense places strains on the economy beyond those expressed in monetary terms.

The Soviet leadership recognizes the high opportunity cost of defense. If economic capacity were standing idle, military expenditures might employ resources that would not otherwise be utilized. However, the Soviet economy operates near full employment, so the defense sector claims scarce resources that are sorely needed in civilian industry. The Soviet leadership seeks to accelerate economic growth by using available resources more efficiently. The defense industry not only drains the civilian sector of skilled labor, materials, and equipment but also utilizes these resources with scant attention to cost-effectiveness.

Furthermore, the burden of the arms race falls disproportionately on the USSR because its economic capacity is far smaller than that of the United States. In order to preserve strategic parity, the Soviet Union must devote a larger share of

GNP to military expenditure than the United States. "In proportional terms," explains Oleg Bykov, deputy director of *IMEMO*, "we have to spend incomparably more on defense than does the other side."[25] The relative disadvantage at which the Soviet Union finds itself in competing militarily with the West puts severe strains on the Soviet economy and impedes economic reform. According to Bykov, "The need to maintain parity even at a constant level will do gigantic damage to our economy. . . . Inordinate nonproductive military expenditures are hindering *perestroika*."[26]

Gorbachev and his advisors, from the moment they took office, intended to bring Soviet defense spending under control. They immediately revised the party's definition of material support for the military. Instead of promising, as the Politburo had done up to 1985, "to provide the Army and Navy with everything they need,"[27] they offered "to give the USSR Armed Forces everything necessary for the reliable defense of our fatherland and its allies."[28] The leadership's interest in easing the defense burden on the economy was shared by military modernists. As early as 1985, First Deputy Chief of the General Staff Makhmut Gareyev noted the need to ensure reliable defense at an affordable cost.[29]

In January 1989, Gorbachev announced plans to reduce the defense budget by 14.2 percent in two years,[30] which would require cuts in military programs beyond those which the USSR had specifically promised to make.[31] He later expressed the intention of lowering by 33–50 percent the share of national income devoted to defense by 1995.[32] In June 1989, Prime Minister Ryzhkov made public a defense budget of 77.3 billion rubles. The largest share, 32.6 billion rubles, is devoted to purchasing armaments and equipment; 15.3 billion rubles is spent on scientific research and experimental design work. The cost of maintaining the army and navy amounts to 20.2 billion rubles, and the remainder covers general military development, pensions, and other items.[33] This defense budget fails to itemize expenditures but offers more credible figures than past budgets and shows the proportion of the main categories of military spending. In 1989, according to the CIA, Soviet defense expenditures declined by 4–5 percent.[34]

By the CIA's calculation, military procurement absorbs about 7–8 percent of GNP and one-third of the output of the machine-building sector.[35] A large volume of weapons production has a damaging effect on industrial growth. High levels of military procurement exacerbate bottlenecks and reduce growth of investment by diverting resources away from the manufacture of producer durables. Limiting investment slows the accumulation and replacement of capital stock, which hampers industrial modernization.[36]

Procurement of weapon systems, the CIA asserts, was the main source of growth in Soviet defense spending in the mid-1980s. Expenditures on naval construction rose sharply, caused primarily by increased spending on submarines. Missile procurement, particularly for ICBMs and strategic surface-to-air missiles, displayed strong growth.[37] Total output of ICBMs, which was very low from 1984 to 1986, returned to levels of the early 1980s. Production of long-range cruise missiles rose by a factor of three after Gorbachev's accession.[38] Recognizing the damaging effect of high military procurement on the defense burden and on the machine building sector, Gorbachev announced plans to cut weapons production more sharply than defense spending as a whole, by 19.5 percent over two years.[39] The CIA estimates that in 1989, procurement outlays dropped 6–7 percent, including a 3 percent decline in procurement of strategic forces.[40]

Military research and development comprise a large part of the country's scientific work. Soviet official statistics, which claim that roughly half of Soviet research and development is devoted to the military,[41] are understated. Roald Sagdeyev, the former director of the Institute for Space Research, suggested that in Moscow, 70 percent of all R&D personnel were employed in the defense sector.[42] The opportunity cost of military research and experimental design work is very high. Military technology tends to offer few applications for civilian industry. The Soviet economy is inept at diffusing new technology, and interaction between military research institutes and their civilian counterparts is minimal. Therefore, innovation in the defense sector has little impact on the rest of the economy. Bykov concluded that "military technology is quite specific, and its contribution to the civilian sphere is insignificant."[43]

The priority claim of the defense sector on scientific resources contributes to the Soviet economy's technological lag behind Western countries. The military-industrial complex holds a virtual monopoly on advanced technology and transfers to the civilian sector only the goods it has rejected.[44] In recognition of this drain on scientific resources, the budget approved by the Supreme Soviet for 1990 cuts appropriations for military research and development by 14.3 percent.[45] Chief of the General Staff Moiseyev stated that "a whole series of experimental design projects" was being stopped.[46]

SAVINGS FROM ARMS CONTROL

Nuclear disarmament offers some immediate benefits, but the large savings accrue over time. The Intermediate- and Short-Range Missile Treaty has released 400 million rubles.[47] The CIA predicts that conclusion of a strategic arms agreement will save the Soviet Union several billion rubles a year.[48] Reductions in nuclear arsenals stimulate conventional force cuts and raise the prospect of substantial dividends resulting from lower levels of tanks, artillery, troops, and aircraft. Even in the absence of formal arms control accords, the easing of East-West tensions strengthens the political groups in the USSR advocating decreased military expenditures and creates a domestic environment conducive to industrial conversion and reform of the defense complex.

Arms reductions provide the near-term benefit of increasing the availability of resources for civilian purposes. Inputs into military research and development and production can be redirected promptly to the civilian economy. Most materials used in weapons production, such as specialty steels, construction materials, and engineering fibers, are readily transferred to the civilian sector. Intermediate goods, such as bearings, composites, and microelectronics, are relatively easy to apply to nonmilitary production and are greatly in demand. Employment of defense industry workers in the civilian sector would provide substantial benefits.[49]

The bulk of the savings from disarmament will be generated over the longer term by conversion of industrial capacity to civilian uses. The defense complex is an experienced manufacturer of civilian products. Military factories have for years put out a wide range of consumer and industrial goods, from refrigerators, bicycles, and samovars to railroad cars, irrigation equipment, computers, and facsimile machines.[50] Civilian output can be raised more rapidly by the defense industry directly than by transferring resources to the civilian sector. Furthermore, military plants are considered to be higher-quality producers than their civilian counterparts. So, practically all announced cases of conversion take place within the defense complex without moving enterprises to the jurisdiction of civilian authorities.[51] Rather than transfer manpower and equipment from defense to civilian factories, the USSR retains them under the control of military-industrial ministries and shifts existing facilities from military to nonmilitary output.[52]

Soviet plans for conversion entail a steady increase in the already established production of civilian goods in defense plants. Ryzhkov announced in 1989 that civilian production, which has accounted for 40 percent of the total output of the defense sector, will increase to 46 percent by 1991 and to more than 60 percent by 1995.[53] The conversion program targets key branches of the economy: agricultural machinery, light industry, trade, public catering, medical equipment, computer technology, electronics, and consumer goods.[54] Igor Belousov, the chairman of the State Military-Industrial Commission, set ambitious targets for raising output of civilian aircraft, electronic equipment, and personal computers.[55]

The government is unlikely to meet its goals for conversion. Defense enterprises assigned to manufacture civilian goods lose their privileged access to inputs and thus experience difficulties in maintaining the same level of output.[56] Many military factories are too specialized to produce consumer durables and industrial goods. They must change their output, disrupting production and incurring additional costs.[57] Although the USSR began in 1989 to undertake conversion in a systematic way, investments into the program were not forthcoming until a year later, when the state promised to defray the costs of retooling plants with funds released by cutbacks in military procurement.[58]

The conversion process is centrally directed and preserves the inefficiencies of the defense industry. The government issues state orders to cover almost the entire output of civilian goods from military plants, so the defense complex ends up manufacturing products that are more expensive than those sold by civilian enterprises.[59] Some Soviet experts want to place converted weapon plants under the authority of civilian ministries[60] and to carry out conversion through market forces with government coordination.[61] They favor the release of high technology from the defense complex and the creation of a civilian sector to develop microelectronics and computers.[62]

Cuts in military spending generate pressure for reform of the defense industry. The USSR spends much more on defense than the United States does to produce the same amount of equipment, because the Soviet industry manufactures high-quality weapons at great cost.[63] The Soviet leadership, therefore, has set out to improve efficiency in the defense sector. The emphasis on quality over quantity in defense made at the 19th Party Conference included calls to render arms production more cost-effective. In line with his demand that "military construction" be "secured through primarily qualitative parameters," Gorbachev affirmed the need "in a short term to create a modern and vigorous industry" including "military plants."[64] Deputy Defense Minister for Armaments Shabanov expressed the belief that military production had yet to realize its full potential.[65]

Military leaders were especially concerned about research and development in the defense sector. Shabanov harshly criticized the slow progress in technological innovation[66] and the sluggish pace at which discoveries were implemented. "The introduction of new developments is generally a weak point in our country and in the Armed Forces in particular," he complained, and "only 20 percent of the inventions are put into operation." Shabanov asserted the conviction that military research often provided a poor source of innovation. "On the average," he noted, "almost 40 percent of the patent applications are disapproved annually because they contain nothing new. And this rejection rate is particularly high in a number of institutes and organizations in the Missile Forces."[67]

To overcome the past practice of improving armaments in small increments, Shabanov called for "radical methods" to increase the technological standards of Soviet weaponry.[68] Sharp improvement in military research and development, Shabanov argued, should be accomplished by using available resources more efficiently and by fostering an open atmosphere in the military R&D community.[69] Defense Minister Yazov underscored the need to apply more swiftly scientific discoveries and technological breakthroughs to weapons development.[70]

At the beginning of 1989, enterprises of the defense industry, including research institutes and design bureaus, became financially accountable. They are expected to grow self-sufficient as a result of military reform. They will bid for contracts with the Defense Ministry, retaining profits and incurring losses, and will sell consumer goods in the open market. They will come under pressure to cut costs or else charge higher prices.[71] Most likely, prices will rise, and the Defense Ministry will constrain the procurement budget by purchasing fewer arms. Restructuring of the military-industrial complex, Yazov explains, is designed to boost the efficiency of arms production and thereby to maintain effective defenses at lower cost. He already has plans to reduce the number of contractors.[72]

Lower levels of weapons procurement, by removing the priority receipt of inputs to military enterprises, disrupt production in the defense industry but ease bottlenecks in the machine-building sector and thereby contribute to growth of civilian output. However, the large savings derive from cuts in the number of new weapon systems. Spending on strategic armaments goes mostly into development, testing, and investment for production capacities. The cost of strategic forces depends mainly on the diversity of new systems put into service and much less on the amount of serial production.[73] Soviet estimates place three-quarters of the possibilities for lowering weapon costs in the developmental phase,[74] so reformers advocate procurement of fewer but better arms. The Supreme Soviet Defense Committee recommends that the defense industry reduce the range of its products, discontinue output of obsolete models, and supply only modern and effective weapons.[75]

Gorbachev and his advisors seek to maintain progress in the reform program by substantially reducing military expenditures under stable international conditions. They plan to raise the rate of Soviet economic growth through improvements in industrial productivity stimulated by inputs of technology from the defense complex. The savings from arms cuts result in part from immediate increases in supplies of materials and intermediate goods but mainly accrue over time following initial investments. A stable international environment helps the Gorbachev leadership to sustain political support for converting industrial capacity to civilian output as well as for restructuring the defense industry.

Disarmament releases economic potential and technological resources primarily by decreasing the number of weapon systems. The most substantial economic benefits are derived from closing down lines of weapons production and reequipping them to manufacture civilian goods. Negotiated agreements eliminate certain categories of weapons and, by lowering arms levels, encourage efforts to reduce the variety of available systems. They enhance predictability in the strategic situation and thereby facilitate force planning so that the USSR can introduce fewer new weapon systems incorporating greater technological improvements.

NOTES

1. *Pravda*, 17 June 1986.
2. *Pravda*, 12 June 1985.
3. *Pravda*, 9 November 1985.
4. *Sovetskaya Rossia*, 17 August 1988.
5. M. Karpunin, "Ekonomicheskiye Problemy Operezhayushchevo Razvitia Mashinostroyenia" ["Economic Problems of the Excelling Development of Machine-Building"], *Planovoye Khozyaystvo* [Planned Economy], January 1988, p. 19.
6. *Sovetskaya Rossia*, 17 August 1988.
7. *Pravda*, 10 July 1988.
8. The number of joint ventures registered rose from 168 in 1988 to 1,083 in 1989, according to *PlanEcon Report*, 21 February 1990, p. 35.
9. *Pravda*, 24 October 1989.
10. I. P. Faminsky and I. D. Ivanov in roundtable discussion, "K Voprosu o Teory Vsemirnovo Khozyaystva" ["To the Question of a Theory of World Economy"] *Mirovaya Ekonomika i Mezhdunarodnye Otnoshenia (MEMO)*, December 1989, pp. 59, 69.
11. U.S. Central Intelligence Agency and Defense Intelligence Agency (CIA/DIA), "The Soviet Economy in 1988: Gorbachev Changes Course," 14 April 1989, p. 1, and "The Soviet Economy Stumbles Badly in 1989," 20 April 1990, Table C-4.
12. *Pravda*, 19 October 1987.
13. *Pravda*, 29 June 1988.
14. *Ekonomicheskaya Gazeta*, no. 36 (September), 1988.
15. *Pravda*, 11 November 1989.
16. *Pravda*, 3 July 1990.
17. Summarized in *Military Balance 1985/86*, (London: International Institute for Strategic Studies, July 1985) pp. 17–20, and *Military Balance 1986/87*, (London: IISS, July 1986) pp. 32–36.
18. Donald F. Burton, "Estimating Soviet Defense Spending," *Problems of Communism*, March/April 1983, vol. 32, no. 2 and Abraham S. Becker, *Sitting on Bayonets* (Santa Monica, CA: RAND, December 1985), pp. 19–22.
19. Franklyn D. Holzman, "Politics and Guesswork: CIA and DIA Estimates of Soviet Military Spending," *International Security*, vol. 14, no. 2 Fall 1989, and James E. Steiner and Franklyn D. Holzman, "Correspondence: CIA Estimates of Soviet Military Spending," *International Security*, vol. 14, no. 4 Spring 1990.
20. U.S. Department of Defense, *Soviet Military Power 1988* (Washington: GPO, 1989), p. 32, and CIA/DIA, "The Soviet Economy in 1988," p. 18.

21. Defense Department, *Soviet Military Power 1989*, p. 32, and, CIA/DIA, "The Soviet Economy in 1988," pp. 1, 15.
22. U.S. Central Intelligence Agency (CIA), *The Soviet Weapons Industry*, September 1986, pp. 4–6.
23. *Izvestia*, 28 April 1990.
24. *Pravda*, 31 May 1989.
25. *Izvestia*, 28 March 1989.
26. Ibid.
27. Andropov in *Pravda*, 23 November 1982; see also Brezhnev in *Pravda*, 28 October 1982.
28. *Pravda*, 24 April 1985; see also *Pravda*, 12 March 1985.
29. Makhmut A. Gareyev, *M. V. Frunze—Voyenny Teoretik* [M. V. Frunze, Military Theorist] (Moscow: Voyenizdat, 1985), p. 425.
30. *Pravda*, 19 January 1989.
31. CIA/DIA, "The Soviet Economy in 1988," p. 18.
32. *Pravda*, 7 July 1989.
33. *Izvestia*, 9 June 1989.
34. CIA/DIA, "The Soviet Economy Stumbles Badly," p. 11.
35. CIA, *The Soviet Weapons Industry*, p. 2.
36. Ibid., p. 8.
37. CIA/DIA, "The Soviet Economy in 1988," p. 15.
38. Defense Department, *Soviet Military Power 1989*, p. 35.
39. *Pravda*, 19 January 1989.
40. CIA/DIA, "The Soviet Economy Stumbles Badly," p. 11–13.
41. The "science" budget amounted to 37.8 billion rubles. *Narodnoye Khozyaystvo SSSR 1988* [The USSR's National Economy 1988], (Moscow: Finansyi Statistika, 1989) p. 275.
42. Roald Sagdeyev, "A Man Who Can Say No," *New Times*, no. 47 (November), 1988, p. 27.
43. *Izvestia*, 28 March 1989.
44. Sergei Yu. Glazyev and Dmitri S. Lvov, "Ostatsya Vcherashnimi?" ["Remain Yesterday's?"] *Kommunist*, no. 8 (May), 1989, p. 23.
45. *Izvestia*, 16 December 1989.
46. *Izvestia*, 23 February 1990.
47. Shevardnadze in *Pravda*, 24 October 1989.
48. CIA/DIA, "The Soviet Economy in 1988," p. 19.
49. Ibid., p. 20.
50. CIA, *The Soviet Weapons Industry*, p. 3.
51. Alexei Izyumov in *Literaturnaya Gazeta*, 12 July 1989.
52. CIA/DIA, "The Soviet Economy in 1988," p. 20.
53. *Izvestia*, 9 June 1989.

54. Igor S. Belousov, "Konversia: Politika i Ekonomika" ["Conversion: Politics and Economics"] *Kommunist Vooruzhennykh Sil*, no. 17 (September), 1989, p. 28 and Ryzhkov in *Pravda*, 14 December 1989.
55. *Moskovskaya Pravda*, 24 October 1989.
56. Izyumov.
57. *Ekonomicheskaya Gazeta*, no. 30 (July), 1989.
58. Belousov in *Pravda*, 7 February 1990.
59. *Krasnaya Zvezda*, 4 April 1990.
60. Alexei Kireyev, "Crawling towards Disarmament," *New Times*, no. 10 (March), 1990, p. 31.
61. Ksenia Gonchar, "Eto Trudnoye Delo—Ekonomika Razoruzhenia" ["It is a Difficult Matter—The Economics of Disarmament"], *Kommunist*, no. 9 (June), 1990, pp. 103–5.
62. Ibid., pp. 103, 106.
63. Ed A. Hewett in "Panel on Growth and Technology in *Perestroyka*," *Soviet Economy*, vol. 3, no. 4, October-December 1987, pp. 347–48.
64. *Pravda*, 29 June 1988.
65. *Krasnaya Zvezda*, 14 August 1988.
66. Ibid.
67. *Krasnaya Zvezda*, 15 November 1988.
68. Ibid.
69. *Krasnaya Zvezda*, 14 August 1988.
70. *Krasnaya Zvezda*, 9 August 1988.
71. *Krasnaya Zvezda*, 19 May 1990.
72. *Krasnaya Zvezda*, 5 June 1990.
73. Alexei Arbatov, "How Much Defense is Sufficient?" *International Affairs*, April 1989, p. 36.
74. *Krasnaya Zvezda*, 19 October 1989.
75. *Krasnaya Zvezda*, 14 October 1989.

3

NEW THINKING ON NATIONAL SECURITY AIMS

Fundamental revisions in Soviet security aims inspired the USSR to pursue a policy of nuclear disarmament. New political thinking redefines Soviet interests, reassesses the nature of the threat facing the USSR, and alters the means for enhancing Soviet security. Gorbachev and his advisors subordinate Soviet global interests to the exigencies of domestic reconstruction because Soviet power is derived first and foremost from economic vigor. Military might, in their view, constitutes an important but diminished source of Soviet strength. The external threat is subsiding, encouraged by Soviet actions. Since Western enmity was partly of Soviet making, modified Soviet behavior generates willingness in the West to forge cooperative relations. The USSR relies increasingly on constructive diplomacy to promote its interests. Disarmament reduces the military component of Soviet security and alleviates world tensions, thereby facilitating Soviet entry into the global economy and international system and fostering Soviet economic modernization.

Changes in Soviet arms control policy are stifled by resistance to the revised security aims. Gorbachev admitted in early 1989 that "the new political thinking is still only in the process of winning minds."[1] Though very few outright opponents retain influence over decision making, a number of leaders, who are on the whole favorably inclined toward new thinking, express reservations about one or another of its aspects. More traditional officials approve of reform and East-West cooperation but appear uncomfortable with the decline in the USSR's world standing. They seek to limit reductions in Soviet armed forces. They refuse to acknowledge Soviet responsibility for aggravating the Western threat, to accept Western rules of interaction or to substitute military might with arms control as the primary means of protecting Soviet interests.

DEFINING NATIONAL INTERESTS

Soviet security, in the view of Gorbachev and his supporters, rests primarily on internal strength. Soviet power stems from the USSR's economic potential and the quality of Soviet life. The security of the Soviet Union can be enhanced most effectively by raising economic output and living standards. The Gorbachev leadership launched domestic reform in order to build a modern economy, with a technologically advanced production base, which is capable of satisfying the material needs of the population and eventually competing in the global market. Economic restructuring requires political reform. The reorganization of government is designed to improve economic management, to provide efficient political administration, and to create an open society. Security policy under Gorbachev is designed to promote the reconstruction of the Soviet system.

The USSR's world role, according to new thinking, is defined by domestic exigencies. Foremost among Soviet global interests is peace. At the 27th Congress of the Communist Party in February 1986, Gorbachev declared that the "main goal" of his international strategy is "to provide the Soviet people with the possibility of working in conditions of lasting peace and freedom."[2] He recognizes, as did his predecessors, the gravity of the nuclear threat. Gorbachev describes nuclear war in stark terms, calling it "senseless" and "irrational" because "there would be neither winners nor losers" and "world civilization would inevitably perish."[3] The danger that nuclear war poses to the survival of humanity is fully appreciated by all members of the Soviet elite.⁴ The Gorbachev leadership, with the backing of the high command, enshrined the prevention of war as a fundamental aim of Soviet military doctrine.⁵ The USSR cannot avert armed conflict through diplomacy alone. It must also restructure Soviet defenses to reduce the risk of war.

Promoting peace requires coexistence of the two social systems, since the ultimate victory of socialism is no longer anticipated for the foreseeable future. Soviet leaders realize that the Western system will survive for many years to come. Capitalism, Chernenko admitted, "possesses considerable and by no means exhausted reserves for development."⁶ Gorbachev reported to the 27th Party Congress that "the present stage of the general crisis is not bringing about the absolute stagnation of capitalism, and it does not rule out the possible growth of its economy."⁷ By mastering the "scientific-technological revolution," capitalism has gained a new lease of life.

New thinking reduces the ideological content of Soviet foreign policy. It channels Soviet rivalry with the West into peaceful areas, abandons class struggle, grants priority to Soviet economic renewal, and prescribes growing interaction with the capitalist system including cooperation to solve global problems. Gorbachev explains that new political thinking "assumes a de-ideologizing of interstate relations" but not "of international relations."⁸ He distinguishes relations between governments, on the one hand, from international relations as a whole on the other. "De-ideologizing" interstate relations means giving precedence to cooperation over competition with foreign governments and living up to the principle of noninterference in the internal affairs of other countries, particularly renouncing "doctrines justifying the export of revolution."⁹ In contrast, international relations retain an ideological basis because the Soviet Union has not "given up the class analysis of the causes of the nuclear threat and of other global problems" (the USSR still blames capitalism for creating tension in the world) and because "economic, political, and ideological competition between capitalist and socialist countries is inevitable." Only now, ideological differences "must be kept within a framework of peaceful competition that necessarily envisages cooperation."[10] Soviet foreign policy must pursue state interests above ideological ones. Relations with the West, which used to be characterized by antagonism, are now governed by pragmatic interaction. The outcome of rivalry between the systems will be determined primarily by their respective economic performance.

According to new thinking, ideological differences must be set aside so that the Soviet Union can concentrate on generating technological and economic growth. The revised Party Program, adopted at the 27th Party Congress, drops the old precept that class conflict extends to interbloc relations. Shevardnadze states explicitly that coexistence "cannot be equated with the class struggle." He goes on to say that in the present era, the "defining tendency" is no longer "the struggle between the two opposing systems" but rather "the ability to use advanced science and high technology to increase material goods at an accelerated pace."[11] Andrei Kozyrev, the head of the Foreign Ministry's International Organizations Department, points out that the question, Which social system will prevail in the end? is largely theoretical, because the USSR presently faces a practical question: As a socialist state, shall we be competitive on the global market with commodities, ideas, and services?[12]

The future of socialism hinges on its ability to master the technological revolution. The Soviet Union must demonstrate its worth by applying the latest scientific developments to create world-class products and services. All of Gorbachev's economic priorities, in his words, add "up to one thing—acceleration of scientific and technological progress."[13] This progress cannot be accomplished in isolation from the rest of the world. The Soviet Union, Gorbachev emphasizes, cannot develop normally outside of the global economy.[14] Growing interaction with the West is imperative for the USSR to restructure its economy and to surmount its technological lag behind industrially advanced countries. Autarky dooms the Soviet Union to a chronic lag, as the USSR tries constantly to catch up with already developed technologies. The Soviet Union can match and possibly surpass global levels of technological progress only by entering the world economy.[15]

The Soviet government plans to reach world standards of living by increasing involvement with the West. As Vadim Medvedev, the party's ideological chief until July 1990, explains, the "paths of development" of socialism and capitalism "inevitably intersect; the two systems inevitably interact."[16] The notion of "global interdependence" connotes Soviet participation in "the worldwide division of labor and resources."[17] Gorbachev told members of the Trilateral Commission that the Soviet Union intends to "integrate itself into the world economy" in "stages" in order to stimulate "scientific and technological progress."[18]

Interaction between the two systems generates more shared interests and increasing similarities. Aleksandr Yakovlev sees convergence growing with the spread of democracy, markets, and information across the globe.[19] Common human development triggers changes in socialism, such as the establishment of the rule of law, that coincide with capitalism and thereby create greater unity of interests.[20] The distinguished political commentator Aleksandr Bovin expects peaceful competition between the two systems (comparing ways of life, political systems, and forms of social and economic organization) to provide a source of self-correction for both socialism and capitalism that eventually will lead them to merge.[21]

Among the Soviet interests held in common with the West is the need to solve global problems. Proponents of new thinking underscore the importance of collaboration in addressing developments that endanger all parts of the globe. The existence of problems that affect socialist and capitalist countries alike, such as the greenhouse effect and the depletion of natural resources, was recognized during the Brezhnev era. However, only in recent years did Soviet leaders accept some share of responsibility for resolving them.[22]

New thinking recognizes that Soviet involvement in the Third World strains relations with the West, particularly the United

States, and drains resources that are badly needed at home. Accordingly, Soviet policy shifted from promoting "the struggle for national liberation" to settling regional conflicts. In the 1970s, new thinkers argue, superpower rivalry for the allegiance of developing countries had degenerated into confrontation, which adversely affected the climate for arms control. The USSR by the 1980s had lost the economic capacity to compete with the West. The Soviet Union under Gorbachev respects the right of Third World states to choose their own path of development and seeks to exert influence mainly through example of successful Soviet development.[23]

New thinkers realize that Soviet expansion fails to conceal domestic weakness and that the internal strength of the USSR will determine its future. As Alexei Izyumov and Andrei Kortunov of the USA Institute explain, "In the final count the outcome of the competition between the two systems is decided not in Nicaragua or Afghanistan but in the main centers of socialism and capitalism."[24] The Gorbachev leadership reexamined Soviet commitments to Third World clients, requested recipient countries to institute reforms in return for economic aid, and substantially curtailed the Soviet military presence. The USSR is removing its troops from most foreign outposts, including Mongolia and Vietnam. It is cooperating with the United States to resolve conflicts from Cambodia to Ethiopia. It joined the world condemnation of Iraq's invasion of Kuwait. Soviet support for the economic boycott of Iraq, beyond its immediate objectives, is meant to demonstrate Soviet readiness to act in unison with the international community at a time when collective security systems in Europe are under discussion.

The cost of propping up neighboring Communist regimes convinced the Soviet Union to relinquish its dominance over Eastern Europe. Gorbachev and his advisors tried to persuade the old generation of leaders to introduce reform in order to strengthen the flagging legitimacy of Communist rule. They hoped to preserve the cohesion of the bloc by retaining the leading role of the Communist Party and membership in the Warsaw Pact.

When the conservative Communists refused to heed to Soviet pressure for reform, Moscow withdrew its support. In May 1989, Shevardnadze made it known that the Brezhnev Doctrine, which justified Soviet invasion of its allies to uphold socialism, no longer applied.[25] The Warsaw Pact's Political Consultative Committee in July proclaimed that "there are no universal socialist models" and recognized "the right of each state to develop its own political policy, strategy, and tactics without outside interference."[26] The ensuing revolutions at the end of the year toppled all of the East European leaders, unseated most of the Communist governments, and initiated the dissolution of the Warsaw Pact.

While proponents of new thinking welcome events in Eastern Europe as a boost for *perestroika*,[27] traditional Soviet Communists are alarmed by what the revolutions portend for their future.[28] Ligachev had challenged Shevardnadze's view on the diminishing ideological content of Soviet foreign policy[29] and in March 1990 warned that the socialist community was falling apart.[30] Gorbachev was accused of "surrendering the positions of socialism" and of "repudiating class approaches and the interests of the national-liberation movement."[31] Critics charged Shevardnadze with abandoning Soviet allies.[32]

Conservatives are disconcerted by the USSR's declining world stature. They argue that class conflict should take precedence over cooperation in Soviet foreign policy and that relations with Western states should be governed by class interests. Critics of new thinking want to preserve solidarity with revolutionaries in developing countries and with Communists in Eastern Europe. They oppose efforts to purchase East-West harmony at the expense of Soviet global prestige.

New thinking downgrades the value of military power. The maintenance of large Soviet armed forces complicates *perestroika*, absorbing resources needed for industrial modernization and impeding the development of cooperative relations with the West. Arms cuts facilitate the accomplishment of domestic tasks and bring the Soviet defense potential back into proportion with the USSR's internal strength.

The past buildup of military might was designed to compensate for Soviet weakness. Before Gorbachev took office, argue Radomir Bogdanov of the Soviet Peace Committee and Andrei Kortunov, the Soviet Union tried to reduce all the diverse forms of competition between the two systems to chiefly military ones and made strategic parity something of a substitute for social and economic achievements.[33] However, the growth of Soviet armed forces failed both to conceal domestic decline and to sustain an increase in political influence. The Soviet Union's power in the 1980s diminished as a result of stagnation at home. The USSR's status in world politics, Bogdanov and Kortunov continue, is bound to diminish irrespective of whether or not it preserves a surplus of nuclear arms, because it falls short of highly developed countries on very many counts, including economic structure, living standards, life expectancy, and the environment.[34]

So long as it is commensurate with the USSR's economic potential, military might remains an important measure of Soviet power. Rather than dismiss the significance of armed force, new thinking sets the goal of bridging the gap between the economy and defense policy[35] or, as Yevgeni Primakov put it, "optimizing" the ratio of military to civilian spending.[36] Soviet defense must be rendered affordable, in both financial and technological terms. Cuts in military expenditure contribute to economic growth, which, in turn, sustains military power. Similarly, the release of scientific resources from the defense sector stimulates technological progress and thereby provides the foundation for creating modern armed forces.

Effective military might, Sergei Blagovolin of *IMEMO* maintains, rests on a technologically advanced economy. He explains that new areas of science, such as superconductivity and computers, are constantly applied to arms production. The breadth of technological change prevents the USSR from compensating for general backwardness with crash programs, as the Soviet Union did in the past to build nuclear weapons and spacecraft. Without a sharp acceleration of the country's overall scientific and technological development, Blagovolin concludes, the Soviet armed forces run the risk of losing their capacity to perform effectively.[37]

Soviet military forces must be structured in a way that most efficiently meets Soviet security needs. Blagovolin advocates cuts in the less essential and more expensive parts of the defense budget. He regards the navy as a prime candidate for substantial reduction, since the USSR, abandoning its aspirations to maintain a global military standing, can relinquish its power projection capabilities. Large cuts in air defenses and manpower are also considered appropriate.[38] Blagovolin favors relatively small armed forces equipped with modern weapons and nuclear arms.[39]

New thinking attaches reduced but continued importance to nuclear weapons. Some reformers stress the diminishing utility of nuclear arsenals. Gorbachev told the United Nations in December 1988 that "as the physical symbol and vehicle of absolute military strength, [nuclear arms] have at the same time laid bare the absolute limits of this strength."[40] The USSR's nuclear potential provides a poor indication of Soviet power, according to Andrei Melville of the USA Institute, because that potential is difficult to put into practice, both in a direct military sense and for achieving political aims.[41]

Gorbachev criticized the concept of nuclear deterrence for aggravating world tensions and stimulating the arms race.[42] The criticism, which was echoed by some new thinkers, is repeated most often by conservatives who consider deterrence a mere excuse for American arms buildup.[43] Many Soviet officials point out the enduring value of nuclear weapons. Alexei Arbatov, the head of *IMEMO*'s disarmament section, opposes large unilateral reductions of strategic forces because of the "political role of nuclear equilibrium."[44] Other civilian strategists uphold the utility of nuclear deterrence in helping to regulate superpower relations and to prevent war.[45] They express concern about the possibility of nuclear disarmament increasing the likelihood of conventional war,[46] especially if the level of conventional arms remains high.[47]

ASSESSING THE THREAT

New thinking alters the assessment of threats to Soviet interests. It recognizes the reduced danger of war and the increased vulnerability arising from economic weakness. The external threat, according to new thinking, is partly of Soviet making and can diminish in response to moderation of Soviet policy. The reevaluation of challenges to Soviet interests is widely shared by decision makers, but occasional dissenting voices are heard reiterating old assumptions about the source and intensity of danger to the USSR.

New thinking discredits the traditional view of capitalism as inherently aggressive. Gorbachev argues that global interdependence can modify the nature of capitalism. Since capitalist and socialist states were allies in World War II, and the whole world currently faces the far greater threat of nuclear catastrophe, then capitalism should prove willing to temper its aggressive tendencies and to collaborate in averting nuclear war. Gorbachev expects capitalism to rid itself of militarism because large defense expenditures stimulated U.S. economic growth in the early postwar years, but today's "supermilitarization" has "resulted in an astronomical state debt and other troubles and defects."[48]

Supporters of Gorbachev elaborate the reasons for the West to modify its defense policy. Capitalism needs to ensure its survival. It restrains its militarism in order to avoid a suicidal nuclear war. As Aleksandr Bovin explains, "Since a frontal clash of capitalism with socialism is fraught with [the danger of] global catastrophe, the instinct of self-preservation begins to work against militarism."[49] Moreover, high military expenditure creates large budget deficits and inflation, which hurt the interests of the entire American ruling class.[50] Capitalist states exhibit different levels of militarism. The example of Japan shows that industrial growth can be sustained by a capitalist economy without a significant amount of defense spending.[51]

The danger of world war breaking out, in the view of new thinkers, is remote. Vitali Zhurkin, director of the Institute of

Europe, argues that there are no conflicts between East and West that could tempt a resort to war. He finds difficulty in imagining what aim could possibly bring Western armies, in a sane mind, to invade the territory of socialist countries.[52] Sergei Blagovolin considers war between the blocs "inconceivable as a conscious act." Aggressive wars of the past were launched with the support of large parts of society in efforts to acquire more living space and resources and thus to resolve domestic problems. Under the present scientific-technological revolution, national prosperity can no longer be equated with territorial size or resource availability. So, Blagovolin concludes, "in no single developed country is there any kind of solid social base for carrying out aggressive actions against the USSR or in general for implementing a policy that could lead to a big war."[53]

The possibility of invasion and the political consequences of Western arms buildup pose less of a threat to Soviet security than the economic impact of weapons competition. Gorbachev affirms the belief that the main objective of imperialism in fueling the arms race is "to exhaust the Soviet Union economically."[54] Vitali Zhurkin explains that the United States notices the large disparity, which arose during the Brezhnev period, between the Soviet Union's global standing and its economic and technological potential. The United States knows that it cannot regain strategic superiority, because the USSR is capable of keeping up in the arms race, but it can use its economic and technological superiority "to achieve success in the struggle of the social systems without war." By compelling the Soviet Union to match all new U.S. weapon programs, at times with measures that are more expensive than the U.S. programs themselves, the United States drags the USSR into an economic rivalry in the hope of driving the Soviet economy to ruin.[55]

The arms race cannot be blamed entirely on the West. Anatoli Dobrynin, then a Central Committee secretary, described the arms race as an action-reaction spiral, implying a certain measure of Soviet responsibility.[56] Gorbachev complained that the Soviet Union allowed itself to be drawn into the arms race.[57] In fact, the growth of Soviet armed forces stimulates intensified Western defense efforts. Alexei Arbatov asserts that "the buildup of the possible enemies' military potential is . . . a process directly influenced by our measures."[58]

The accumulation of Soviet military power, rather than making the United States and Western Europe more responsive to Soviet interests, encountered resistance. Izyumov and Kortunov note the failure of the USSR in the 1970s and early 1980s to translate military might into international influence. Political gains from deployments of Soviet weapons, they observe, began to dwindle and in some cases to undermine Soviet positions in the world. This was especially true in Europe. Despite the substantial expansion of Soviet nuclear and conventional forces in the theater and the fact that never before the turn of the decade had the military balance in Europe been so favorable to the USSR, Soviet influence waned and major Soviet political moves misfired. "The buildup of Soviet military potential led to a closer cohesion of West European countries and the United States."[59]

Past Soviet actions, advocates of new thinking confess, contributed to the threat facing the USSR by provoking hostility in the West and persuading Western countries to band together in opposition. Vyacheslav Dashichev, a leading diplomatic historian, argues that the endeavor of one state to expand sharply its sphere of influence upsets the political balance and causes other countries to unite in an "anticoalition" to restore equilibrium. Washington used the idea of the "Soviet military threat" to ensure its dominance in various parts of the world, and "ill-considered actions" of the Soviet Union gave the United States a pretext for committing acts of aggression and introducing new weapon systems. Dashichev mentions, without rebutting, the Western belief that "the Soviet leadership actively took advantage of détente to build up its military forces, striving for military parity with the United States and with all the opposing powers combined." Soviet behavior sparked the Western reaction of uniting the spiritual and material resources of the capitalist world against the Soviet Union. He concludes that the "great exacerbation of tension in the USSR's relations with the West in the late 1970s and early 1980s" could have been averted. The situation "was caused mainly by errors and the incompetent approach of the Brezhnev leadership."[60]

Western policy toward the USSR is, to a considerable degree, a function of Soviet behavior. Bogdanov and Kortunov propound the opinion that the intensity of anti-Soviet sentiment in American society and the U.S. political leadership is "largely conditioned by the international activity and military construction of the Soviet Union."[61] Since Soviet expansion, arrogant diplomacy, and arms buildup stimulated American hostility, Soviet moderation can inspire restraint on the part of the United States.

Some members of the Soviet elite, especially of the armed forces, were doubtful about Western readiness to renounce aggressive policies and about the ability of the USSR to influence U.S. actions. They warned that militarism remained the defining tendency of imperialist policy and the basis of Western leaders' thinking.[62] They identified imperialism as the source of aggression. Defense Minister Yazov blamed the West, particularly the United States, for instigating the arms race.[63] Another skeptic explained that whenever the United States introduced a new weapon system, the Soviet Union replied by proposing its elimination, and only after the United States refused to ban the new system did the USSR deploy its own version.[64]

The military leadership in 1989 modified its threat assessment. Yazov has admitted that the USSR could have done more to avoid involvement in the arms race[65] and endorsed the political leadership's view that the danger of war has receded. He has stopped ascribing full responsibility for that danger to the West. He expresses the conviction that the deployment on both sides of large groupings of armed forces, maintained at advanced states of combat readiness, contains within itself the risk of conflict.[66] Chief of the General Staff Moiseyev agrees that tension arises from the high level of armaments facing each other, though he sees the threat to Soviet security emanating primarily from NATO and the United States. "The two military-political alliances," he explains, "have created an enormous mutual threat that is exacerbated by the West's military-political actions."[67] The high command emphasizes that the military danger to the Soviet Union remains. Before Western leaders met in London in July 1990 to reexamine alliance strategy, Moiseyev complained that neither NATO doctrine nor its military activity was changing,[68] and Yazov observed that the West "was in no great hurry to renounce inflammatory scenarios of nuclear deterrence" or "direct confrontation."[69] The United States, argued Gorbachev's aide Marshal Akhromeyev, "continues to act largely as before in the military sphere."[70]

PROTECTING SOVIET SECURITY

New thinking maintains that Soviet security can best be protected by strengthening the Soviet economy and fostering cooperative relations with the West. The USSR can promote its national interests by reducing reliance on military power. Cuts in defense release resources for civilian reconstruction and remove impediments to interaction with the United States and Western Europe. The new thinking is garnering increasing support, but some officials remain skeptical of the ability of arms control to compensate for military might in safeguarding Soviet security.

The primary means to further Soviet interests, according to new thinking, lies in revitalizing the Soviet economy. Gorbachev told the 27th Party Congress that economic "dynamism" is needed for ensuring "the peoples' well being," for "counteracting the danger of war," and for demonstrating "the possibilities of the socialist way of life."[71] His supporters explain that the decline in Soviet power, which resulted from economic stagnation, falling living standards and growing technological backwardness, must be reversed by restructuring the Soviet system in line with the scientific-technological revolution.[72] The primary aim of Soviet diplomacy, Shevardnadze declares, is to create external conditions conducive to internal reform.[73] Economic growth generates the resources with which to raise living standards and to sustain military power. Imparting vigor to the Soviet economy strengthens the USSR internally and enhances Soviet authority abroad.

Providing an attractive model of development for other countries contributes to Soviet security. Aleksandr Bovin asserts that the inability of "Communist parties in the capitalist countries and the third world" to "gain the support of the majority of the working class" was due in part to "failures" of the Soviet Union. "Socialism has not yet been able to acquire the force of example." If domestic restructuring is carried out, then the USSR "can not only tell of the new civilization's advantages, but demonstrate them as well" and thereby "make possible a reduction in international tensions . . . and the achievement of social progress in the least painful fashion."[74]

The Soviet Union's global standing, in the view of new thinking, is determined first and foremost by its internal strength. As the collapse of détente demonstrated, military power fails to render the West more accommodating to Soviet interests when Soviet domestic weakness is apparent. The expansion and exercise of the USSR's military potential breeds antagonism on the part of the United States and Western Europe. The Soviet buildup of strategic power, imperious diplomacy, and advances in the Third World provoked a stern Western reaction that left both sides feeling less secure. Undue emphasis on military might proves counterproductive because, as new thinking acknowledges, Soviet behavior does affect Western decisions on security. The USSR's weapon deployments encourage similar responses from the other side. Soviet expansion persuades capitalist states to band closer together. For this reason, Shevardnadze criticized the view "that the Soviet Union can be just as strong as any possible coalition of opposing states."[75] Soviet efforts to acquire that strength trigger a hostile Western response. In contrast, diplomacy discourages the Western introduction of new weapon systems and helps to prevent opposing coalitions from forming.

New thinking prescribes the "achievement of security mainly through political means." Normalizing relations with Western countries, Gorbachev remarks, impairs anti-Soviet sentiment and thereby weakens Western pressure against socialism.[76] Political solutions to security problems tend to be cheaper and more effective than purely military ones, because they forestall possible countermeasures to Soviet actions and temper Western antagonism. Arms agreements can enhance strategic stability by allaying American fears of Soviet weapons and dissuading the United States from deploying new forces of its own. Diplomacy can ensure that the USSR has no enemies and thus has less need for defenses, Shevardnadze notes.[77] Arms control is more urgent for the Soviet Union than the United States because the USSR is in a weaker position to carry on the arms race.[78]

The Gorbachev leadership embraces the principle of "mutual" or "common security." Since security cannot be achieved entirely at the expense of others, a "balance of interests" must be found. The Soviet Union feels safe only if those around it do. Gorbachev asserts that lessened security for the United States is disadvantageous for the Soviet Union, since it engenders mistrust and instability.[79] Therefore, relations with the West require "consideration of one another's legitimate interests," as the revised Party Program of 1986 declares.[80] Flexible diplomacy is crucial. Soviet initiatives must accommodate the concerns of negotiating partners. "We understand that, no matter how important and significant our proposals are, no matter how devoted to them we are, we will not be able to do everything by ourselves," Gorbachev explains. "We work out our proposals while studying and taking into consideration the viewpoints and initiatives of other governments and public and political movements . . . [and] we by no means regard them as final and not open to discussion."[81]

The concepts of safeguarding security by political methods and of mutual security have gained wide currency but still incur criticism. Some Soviet officials, notably in the armed forces, continue to believe that military power is essential for defending Soviet interests and that the West takes advantage of Soviet concessions. They contend that the absence of an effective political mechanism to avert war requires the Soviet Union to rely primarily on military force to hold back aggression,[82] and point out "the exceptionally large role" that "the combat efficiency of our army has in maintaining peace" and defending socialism.[83] With the United States striving to use its technological preponderance to gain strategic superiority, they argue, a high state of readiness of the armed forces is essential to stop encroachments on Soviet sovereignty.[84] The former commander of Soviet forces in Afghanistan, Colonel General Gromov, asserts that political mechanisms to avert war are only beginning to be formed.[85]

In the opinion of conservative elements, Western states still exhibit aggressive tendencies and cannot be expected to show restraint. Regardless of what the Soviet Union does, the West acts in a threatening manner. Soviet compromise appears as weakness to the West and thus encourages menacing Western behavior. When the Soviet Union tries to accommodate Western interests, the West, instead of responding in kind, takes advantage of the USSR. Thus, critics of new thinking raise doubts about the wisdom of compensating with political measures, such as arms control, for military power in protecting Soviet security. They observe influential political forces in NATO and the United States openly opposed to arms reductions[86] and affirm the conviction that even after the USSR puts forward peaceful initiatives, the United States continues to seek unilateral advantages in disarmament negotiations.[87] They express apprehension about the Soviet Union giving up more arms than the United States[88] and about disarmament undermining Soviet defense capabilities.[89] Gromov fears that the arms control process might be reversed,[90] and Moiseyev accuses the West of striving for one-sided gains in the arms talks.[91]

In spite of the skepticism about new thinking, a consensus was formed in favor of arms reduction. Although reluctant at first, the military joined the political leadership in seeking to lower the level of armaments. In February 1987, then defense minister Sokolov endorsed the objective of decreasing military potentials.[92] The Soviet high command expected arms cuts to encompass strategic arsenals. It continued to downgrade the importance of nuclear arms. Strategic nuclear forces had traditionally been considered the main component of Soviet combat might and the basic factor deterring aggression.[93] Military pronouncements of recent years reduced the emphasis on nuclear weapons. Sokolov in March 1986 issued the last statement by a top military official to single out nuclear arms as the mainstay of Soviet defense capabilities.[94]

Proponents of new thinking strive to lower military potentials for political, military, and economic reasons. Arms reductions counteract the decline in Soviet power, ensuring that the shift in the balance of power in favor of the West does not threaten Soviet security.[95] They also remove impediments to cooperative relations with the West and to Soviet participation in the global economy. High levels of armaments, Gorbachev acknowledges, obstruct the inclusion of the USSR in Europe's political and economic development.[96] Cuts in the Soviet Union's military capabilities quell Western fears and thereby facilitate growing Soviet interaction with Western Europe and the United States.

Reduction in the size of armed forces helps to constrain combat capabilities. Gorbachev identifies the qualitative improvement of weaponry as the most dangerous part of the arms race.[97] His supporters point out that the development of military technology can upset the strategic balance even if parity remains intact and therefore that strategic arsenals must be cut.[98] The United States, they observe, is striving for technological superiority[99] and might, in spite of numerical equivalence in nuclear arms, acquire the capacity to launch a disarming first strike.[100] They foresee the deployment in the mid-1990s of a new generation of weapons that, even with low numerical ceilings, would impose an unnecessary cost on the superpowers and could have a destabilizing effect on the nuclear balance.[101] The lowering of arms levels facilitates control of the introduction of new weapon systems.

New thinking recognizes that military power is increasingly a function of the sophistication, as opposed to the number, of arms. By decreasing the size of the Soviet nuclear arsenal, resources can be devoted to improving the quality of remaining weapons.[102] Military modernists want to render Soviet armed forces leaner and more sophisticated. They believe that the effectiveness of the USSR's combat potential is preserved primarily by keeping pace with technological advancements in U.S. weaponry, and therefore that efforts should be concentrated on building modern weapon systems. Producing Soviet arms in large numbers involves an unnecessary expense and provides inadequate compensation for their relatively poor quality. An emphasis on quantitative indicators, Yazov asserts, is becoming increasingly costly and less effective in military terms,[103] so, he says, the Soviet Union must concentrate on improving quality to create slimmer but more capable armed forces.[104]

Cuts in strategic stockpiles can release resources for civilian industry. Advocates of new thinking hope to ease the defense burden by redefining Soviet military requirements according to the principle of "reasonable sufficiency," by relinquishing attempts to emulate Western arms programs. In their view, the United States, expecting the USSR to make symmetrical responses to American steps in the arms race, deliberately tries to exhaust the USSR economically. The Soviet Union can foil these American moves by reducing its defenses to a level of sufficiency.[105] Soviet endeavors to match Western defense programs are particularly expensive because they permit the West to set the terms of military rivalry, to pit Western strengths against Soviet weaknesses, argue new thinkers such as Vitali Zhurkin. The Soviet Union can compete more effectively by concentrating efforts in areas of its advantage.[106] Civilian strategists oppose symmetrical responses to American deployments of nuclear weapons because of differences they perceive in U.S. and Soviet strategic concepts. Alexei Arbatov contends that the procurement of nuclear arms analogous to those of the United States contravenes the "principle of defensive adequacy," since American systems are designed to launch a first strike, whereas Soviet weapons are needed only for retaliation.[107]

Proponents of new thinking see little military use in preserving nuclear parity. Soviet security, according to Arbatov, requires not "equality of military potentials" but rather nuclear weaponry sufficient to inflict unacceptable damage on an aggressor with a second strike. He mentions "some estimates" that "400 megaton-class nuclear charges" would be enough for this purpose.[108] His colleague, Georgi Kunadze, proposes cuts to about 10-20 percent of the USSR's present stockpile.[109] Zhurkin agrees that a small part of the existing nuclear arsenal would be adequate to deter a U.S. attack, but specifies that sufficiency, instead of signifying a set level of weaponry, connotes a dynamic process of unilateral and bilateral force cuts that follows changes in the strategic situation.[110] As the Soviet Union reduces the size of its nuclear arsenal, it must make certain that Western deployments do not undermine Soviet retaliatory capabilities.

The objective of deep cuts in nuclear weapons enjoys staunch support among civilian strategists and considerable political backing. The findings of the report issued in April 1987 by the Committee of Soviet Scientists for Peace on enhancing strategic stability through reductions to 75 percent and then 95 percent of present nuclear arms levels[111] received the endorsement of Gorbachev.[112] In July 1989, Gorbachev reiterated support for minimum deterrence.[113] There even are calls for the Soviet Union to follow the path of nuclear disarmament alone and to achieve minimum deterrence through drastic unilateral cuts in the Soviet nuclear arsenal.[114] However, proponents of new thinking generally oppose large unilateral reductions in strategic arms[115] and favor a roughly equal balance of Soviet and American military potentials.[116]

The leadership of the Soviet armed forces is determined to preserve strategic parity. It approves of arms reductions, but only if conducted on a bilateral basis. Although Yazov calls on the USSR to avoid extensive duplication of Western weapon programs,[117] he insists that Soviet military preparations should be commensurate with the Western threat and that disarmament should be a reciprocal process. Both Yazov and Moiseyev regard parity as the "decisive factor" in preventing war.[118] They declare that the USSR cannot permit the West to attain military superiority, that therefore Soviet defense efforts must take into account those of the West, and that the extent of arms reductions depends on the policies of the United States and NATO.[119] The Soviet Union, Yazov states, must consider Western arms programs when implementing military reform,[120] and Moiseyev demands that further Soviet defense cuts be contingent upon the West's willingness to decrease its armed forces.[121] The high command concedes that Soviet attempts to emulate Western weapon systems are undesirable, and has acquiesced in unilateral arms control measures, but is resolved to retain approximate parity of nuclear potentials.

Differences over Soviet security aims give rise to disagreement over the amount of restraint the USSR should exercise. Critics of new thinking warn that arms control provides a poor substitute for defense. They see Soviet interests threatened predominantly by imperialism as the source of aggression and initiator of the arms race. Western motives remain suspicious, and the American commitment to disarmament is doubtful. Soviet concessions cannot be expected to temper Western antagonism toward socialism. Soviet accommodation, instead of encouraging American moderation, invites the United States to take advantage of the USSR. Arms control offers a useful means of strengthening strategic stability provided that it complements strong defenses. Conservative elements accept accords on weapons reduction that place equal constraints on both sides and admit that compromise is necessary, but only insofar as it elicits corresponding concessions from the United States.

As skepticism about Western intentions diminishes, the Soviet Union demonstrates willingness to make increasingly substantial cuts in nuclear arsenals. The most effective way of raising the Soviet Union's world status, according to new thinking, is to improve Soviet economic performance, specifically to master the technological revolution in cooperation with the West. Close interaction with Western economies and societies allows the USSR to benefit directly from Western achievements and to exert greater political influence abroad. Disarmament diverts part of the national wealth to industrial modernization, realigning Soviet military power with the USSR's economic potential, and removes obstacles to Soviet involvement in the international system, thereby enhancing Soviet security.

Western readiness to respond in kind to Soviet moderation provides ample reason to replace unilateral military methods of protecting Soviet interests with diplomacy and arms control. The Brezhnev leadership's insensitivity to Western concerns and buildup of strategic forces sparked hostility in the United States and Western Europe and furnished a justification for American and NATO deployments of new weapon systems. Modified Soviet behavior under Gorbachev induces restraint from the West. Capitalism is capable of curbing its aggressive tendencies and militaristic impulses, and is encouraged to do so by an accommodating Soviet policy. Showing consideration for Western interests makes the West feel more secure and less inclined to threaten Soviet security. Soviet arms reductions serve to alleviate Western concerns and thus to enable East-West cooperation to develop.

New thinking prescribes substantial Soviet compromise to achieve disarmament. The USSR, reformers believe, should redress its insecurity through political means and avoid antagonizing the United States so that both countries can strengthen their security. Crafting a stable balance of interests reduces the incentives to resort to unilateral military actions that provoke countermeasures from the other side and generate a spiral of hostility. Nuclear arms control enhances Soviet security when the USSR makes genuine concessions to satisfy American concerns. Thus, Gorbachev and his advisors take great care to frame disarmament proposals in such a way that they provide a basis for agreement with the United States.

NOTES

1. *Pravda*, 8 January 1989.
2. *Pravda*, 26 February 1986.
3. Mikhail S. Gorbachev, *Perestroika* (London: Collins, 1987), p. 141.

4. For instance, Sergei Akhromeyev, "Prevoskhodstvo Sovetskoy Voyennoy Nauki i Sovetskovo Voyennvo Iskusstva—Odin iz Vazhneyshikh Faktorov Pobedy v Velikoy Otechestvennoy Voyne" ["Superiority of Soviet Military Science and Soviet Military Art—One of the Most Important Factors for Victory in the Great Patriotic War"], *Kommunist*, no. 3 (February), 1985, p. 60, and Dmitri T. Yazov, *Na Strazhe Sotsializma i Mira* [*On Guard for Socialism and Peace*] (Moscow: Voyenizdat, 1987), p. 30.

5. Yazov in *Krasnaya Zvezda*, 28 July 1987.

6. *Pravda*, 26 April 1984, quoted in Allen Lynch, *The Soviet Study of International Relations* (New York: Cambridge University Press, 1987), pp. 1-2.

7. *Pravda*, 26 February 1986.

8. *Pravda*, 8 January 1989.

9. *Pravda*, 6 April 1989.

10. Gorbachev, *Perestroika*, p. 148.

11. *Pravda*, 26 July 1988.

12. "Novoye Myshleniye v Mezhdunarodnykh Delakh" ["New Thinking in International Affairs"], roundtable discussion, *Kommunist*, no. 8 (May), 1989, p. 105.

13. Gorbachev, *Perestroika*, p. 27.

14. *Pravda*, 8 December 1988.

15. Sergei Yu. Glazyev and Dmitri S. Lvov, "Ostatsya Vcherashnimi?" ["Remain Yesterday's?"], *Kommunist*, no. 8 (May), 1989, pp. 19-21.

16. *Pravda*, 5 October 1988.

17. Gorbachev in *Pravda*, 3 November 1987.

18. *Pravda*, 19 January 1989.

19. *Pravda*, 23 June 1990.

20. "Novoye Myshleniye v Mezhdunarodnykh Delakh," p. 101.

21. Ibid., pp. 99, 101-02.

22. Margot Light, *The Soviet Theory of International Relations* (Brighton, Sussex: Wheatsheaf, 1988), p. 299.

23. Andrei Kozyrev and Andrei Shumikhin, "East and West in the Third World," *International Affairs*, March 1989, pp. 64-70.

24. Alexei Izyumov and Andrei Kortunov, "The Soviet Union in the Changing World," *International Affairs*, August 1988, p. 55.

25. *Time*, 15 May 1989, p. 32.

26. *Pravda*, 9 July 1989.

27. Mikhail Bezrukov and Andrei Kortunov, "Who's in the Vanguard Today?" *New Times*, no. 4 (January), 1990, p. 16, and Sergei A. Karaganov, "The Year of Europe: a Soviet View," *Survival*, vol. 32, no. 2, March/April 1990, p. 122.

28. Seweryn Bialer, "The Passing of the Soviet Order?" *Survival*, vol. 32, no. 2, March/April 1990, p. 112.

29. *Pravda*, 6 August 1988.
30. *Pravda*, 18 March 1990.
31. *Pravda*, 8 January 1989.
32. *Pravda*, 11 July 1990.
33. Radomir Bogdanov and Andrei Kortunov, "On the Balance of Power," *International Affairs*, August 1989, p. 6.
34. Ibid., p. 13.
35. Izyumov and Kortunov, p. 53.
36. *Pravda*, 8 January 1988.
37. Sergei Ye. Blagovolin, "Voyennaya Moshch—Skolko, Kakaya, Zachem?" ["Military Might—How Much, Which, For What?"], *MEMO*, August 1989, pp. 14–15.
38. Ibid., pp. 7, 10–12.
39. Sergei Ye. Blagovolin, "Geopoliticheskiye Aspekty Oboronitelnoy Dostatochnosti" ["Geopolitical Aspects of Defensive Sufficiency"], *Kommunist*, no. 4 (March), 1990, p. 119.
40. *Pravda*, 8 December 1988.
41. Andrei Melville, "Nuclear Revolution and the New Way of Thinking," in Anatoli Gromyko and Martin Hellman (eds.), *Breakthrough* (New York: Walker, 1988), p. 179.
42. *Pravda*, 31 March 1987.
43. Vitali A. Strebkov, "Novaya Model Bezopasnosti: Voyenny Aspekt" ["A New Model of Security: the Military Aspect"], *Kommunist Vooruzhennykh Sil*, no. 2 (January), 1990, p. 24.
44. Alexei Arbatov, "Parity and Reasonable Sufficiency," *International Affairs*, October 1988, pp. 83–84.
45. Ednan Agayev, "Towards a New Model of Strategic Stability," *International Affairs*, March 1989, p. 97, and Genrikh Trofimenko, "Towards a New Quality of Soviet-American Relations," *International Affairs*, December 1988, p. 21. See also opinion poll of Soviet experts on international affairs, Andrei Yu. Melville and Aleksandr I. Nikitin, "Sovetskiye Eksperty o Mirovoy Politike" ["Soviet Experts on World Politics"], *SShA: Ekonomika, Politika, Ideologia* [USA: Economics, Politics, Ideology], June 1989, p. 17.
46. Vladimir P. Lukin, "Na Poroge Novovo Veka" [At the Threshold of a New Age], *MEMO*, December 1987, p. 62.
47. Yuri Ya. Kirshin, "Politika i Voyennaya Strategia v Yaderny Vek" ["Politics and Military Strategy in the Nuclear-Age"], *MEMO*, November 1988, p. 44.
48. *Pravda*, 3 November 1987.
49. Aleksandr Bovin, "Novoye Myshleniye—Trebovaniye Yadernovo Veka" ["New Thinking—The Demand of the Nuclear Age"], *Kommunist*, no. 10 (July), 1986, p. 120.

50. Georgi Arbatov, "Militarizm i Sovremennoye Obshchestvo" ["Militarism and Contemporary Society"], *Kommunist*, no. 2 (January), 1987, p. 114.
51. Yevgeni Primakov, "Kapitalizm vo Vzaimosvyazannom Mire" ["Capitalism in an Interdependent World"], *Kommunist*, no. 13 (September), 1987, p. 106.
52. Vitali V. Zhurkin, Sergei A. Karaganov and Andrei V. Kortunov, "Vyzovy Bezopasnosti—Starye i Novye" ["Challenges of Security—Old and New"], *Kommunist*, no. 1 (January), 1988, p. 44.
53. Blagovolin, "Voyennaya Moshch," p. 9.
54. *Pravda*, 29 July 1986.
55. Zhurkin, Karaganov and Kortunov, "Vyzovy Bezopasnosti," pp. 47–49.
56. Anatoli Dobrynin, "Za Bezyaderny Mir, Navstrechu XXI Veka" ["For a Nuclear-Free World, to Meet the 21st Century"], *Kommunist*, no. 9 (June), 1986, p. 20.
57. *Pravda*, 29 June 1988.
58. Alexei Arbatov, "How Much Defense is Sufficient?" *International Affairs*, April 1989, p. 35.
59. Izyumov and Kortunov, "Soviet Union in the Changing World," pp. 49–50.
60. *Literaturnaya Gazeta*, 18 May 1988.
61. Bogdanov and Kortunov, "Balance of Power," p. 9.
62. Col. P. Skorodenko, "Voyenno-Strategichesky Paritet kak Faktor Nedopushchenia Voyny" ["Military-Strategic Parity as a Factor Averting War"], *Kommunist Vooruzhennykh Sil*, no. 12 (June), 1988, p. 42.
63. Dmitri T. Yazov, *Verny Otchizne* [Faithful to the Fatherland] (Moscow: Voyenizdat, 1988), p. 278.
64. Maj. Gen. Yu. Lyubimov, "O Dostatochnosti Oborony i Nedostatke Kompetentnosti" ["On Defense Sufficiency and Inadequacy of Competence"], *Kommunist Vooruzhennykh Sil*, no. 16 (August), 1989, p. 24.
65. Dmitri T. Yazov, "Novaya Model Bezopasnosti i Vooruzhennye Sily" ["A New Model of Security and the Armed Forces"], *Kommunist*, no. 18 (December), 1989, p. 62.
66. *Izvestia*, 21 April 1989.
67. *Pravda*, 13 March 1989.
68. *Krasnaya Zvezda*, 7 July 1990.
69. *Pravda*, 5 July 1990.
70. *Sovetskaya Rossia*, 12 May 1990.
71. *Pravda*, 26 February 1986.
72. Karaganov, "Year of Europe," pp. 122, 124.
73. *Literaturnaya Gazeta*, 18 April 1990.
74. *Izvestia*, 11 July 1987.

75. *Pravda*, 26 July 1988.
76. *Pravda*, 19 February 1988.
77. *Pravda*, 5 July 1990.
78. Shevardnadze in *Pravda*, 26 June 1990.
79. *Pravda*, 22 November 1985.
80. Revised Party Program, Part 3, Section 3.
81. *Pravda*, 19 August 1986.
82. Skorodenko, "Voyenno-Strategichesky Paritet," pp. 41, 46, and Lt. Gen. Avn. V. Serebryannikov, "Bezopasnost Gosudarstva v Yaderny Vek" ["Security of the State in the Nuclear Age"], *Kommunist Vooruzhennykh Sil*, no. 9 (May), 1988, p 36.
83. V. Serebryannikov, "Predotvrashcheniye Voyny: Vklad Army" ["War Prevention: The Army's Contribution"], *Kommunist Vooruzhennykh Sil*, no. 17 (September), 1989, p. 23.
84. Boris V. Molostov, "Zashchita Otechestva: Novoye Kachestvo" ["Defense of the Fatherland: A New Quality"], *Kommunist Vooruzhennykh Sil*, no. 20 (October), 1989, pp. 16–18.
85. B. Gromov, "Sovetskiye Vooruzhennye Sily: Novoye Kachestvo" ["Soviet Armed Forces: A New Quality"], *Pod Znamenem Leninizma* [Under the Banner of Leninism], no. 2 (January), 1990, p. 32.
86. Skorodenko, "Voyenno-Strategichesky Paritet," p. 44.
87. Lyubimov, "O Dostatochnosti Oborony," p. 24.
88. Mentioned by Shevardnadze in *Pravda*, 24 October 1989.
89. According to Gorbachev, *Pravda*, 6 February 1990.
90. Gromov, "Sovetskiye Vooruzhennye Sily."
91. Address to the 28th Party Congress, *Krasnaya Zvezda*, 7 July 1990.
92. *Pravda*, 23 February 1987.
93. Nikolai Ogarkov in *Krasnaya Zvezda*, 9 May 1984.
94. *Pravda*, 2 March 1986.
95. Karaganov, "Year of Europe," p. 125.
96. *Pravda*, 7 July 1989.
97. *Pravda*, 2 September 1985.
98. Izyumov and Kortunov, "Soviet Union in the Changing World," p. 50.
99. Andrei A. Kokoshin and Valentin V. Larionov, *Predotvrashcheniye Voyny: Doktriny, Kontseptsy, Perspektivy* [War Prevention: Doctrines, Concepts, Prospects] (Moscow: Progress, 1990), p. 20.
100. Lev S. Semeyko, "Razumnaya Dostatochnost—Put k Nadezhnomu Miru" ["Reasonable Sufficiency—The Path to a Safe World"], *Kommunist*, no. 7 (May), 1989, p. 114.
101. Alexei G. Arbatov, "Glubokoye Sokrashcheniye Strategicheskykh Vooruzheny" ["Deep Reduction of Strategic Arms"], *MEMO*, May 1988, pp. 28–29.

102. Arbatov, "Parity and Reasonable Sufficiency," p. 84.
103. *Krasnaya Zvezda*, 9 August 1988.
104. *Krasnaya Zvezda*, 5 June 1990.
105. Yevgeni Primakov in *Pravda*, 10 July 1987.
106. Vitali V. Zhurkin, Sergei A. Karaganov and Andrei V. Kortunov, "O Razumnoy Dostatochnosti" ["On Reasonable Sufficiency"], *SShA*, December 1987, pp. 16–17.
107. Arbatov, "Parity and Reasonable Sufficiency," p. 84.
108. Ibid., pp. 76, 83.
109. Georgi F. Kunadze, "Ob Oboronnoy Dostatochnosti Voyennovo Potentsiala SSSR" ["On Defensive Sufficiency of the USSR's Military Potential"], *MEMO*, October 1989, pp. 68–69.
110. Zhurkin, Karaganov and Kortunov, "O Razumnoy Dostatochnosti," pp. 14–15, 17.
111. Roald Sagdeyev and Andrei Kokoshin (eds.), *Strategic Stability under the Conditions of Radical Nuclear Arms Reductions* (Moscow: April 1987).
112. *Pravda*, 17 September 1987.
113. *Pravda*, 7 July 1989.
114. Bogdanov and Kortunov, "Balance of Power," pp. 7–8.
115. For example Semeyko, "Razumnaya Dostatochnost," p. 114.
116. Melville and Nikitin, "Sovetskiye Eksperty," p. 14.
117. *Krasnaya Zvezda*, 5 June 1990.
118. Yazov, "Novaya Model Bezopasnosti," p. 62, and Moiseyev in *Krasnaya Zvezda*, 7 July 1990.
119. Yazov, *Verny Otchizne*, pp. 288–89, and Mikhail Moiseyev, "Reduction of Armed Forces and Armaments—a Guarantee of Security for All," *International Affairs*, September 1989, p. 9.
120. *Pravda*, 27 June 1990.
121. Mikhail A. Moiseyev, "Problemy Volnuyushchiye Vsekh" ["Problems Worrying Everyone"], *Kommunist Vooruzhennykh Sil*, no. 11 (June), 1990, p. 12.

4

CHANGES IN NUCLEAR STRATEGY

Soviet interest in substantially reducing nuclear arsenals emanates from the demands of new thinking to cut the USSR's military potential. The content of Soviet arms control policy is shaped to a great extent by changes in nuclear strategy. Doctrinal revisions that preceded Gorbachev's accession, and the two-year review of military doctrine undertaken by the Defense Council in April 1985, altered Soviet force requirements and thereby shifted the Soviet position on restricting particular weapon systems. The Gorbachev leadership attaches great value to strategic stability and so reduces first-strike arms in favor of survivable forces appropriate for retaliation.

Disagreements over nuclear strategy stifle Soviet progress in disarmament. The high command of the Soviet armed forces assumes responsibility not only for enhancing stability but also for preparing to carry out military missions in case war breaks out. It is thus determined to preserve some elements of a war-fighting capability, such as counterforce nuclear targeting, that inhibit improvements in strategic stability. In contrast, reform-minded civilian strategists want to render the nuclear balance more durable by decreasing the military utility of nuclear weapons.

Acceptance of mutual vulnerability intensified Soviet efforts to block the development and deployment of ballistic missile defenses. The adoption of a no-first-use doctrine encouraged the

Soviet Union to reduce its first-strike offensive nuclear arms. The heightened interest of the Soviet military in survivable forces prompted a shift of emphasis from land-based missiles to long-range bombers. Civilian experts, keen to improve stability, pressed for cuts in strategic warheads. Elimination of intermediate- and short-range missiles and proposals to reduce tactical nuclear weapons are designed to strengthen the military balance in Europe.

BLOCKING STRATEGIC DEFENSE

The Soviet leadership from the 1970s has maintained a consistent line against the creation of large-scale antiballistic missile (ABM) systems. The achievement of strategic parity reinforced Soviet determination to prevent any reduction in U.S. vulnerability and consequently in Soviet strategic gains. In spite of some Soviet ABM activity, as a means to hedge against the U.S. Strategic Defense Initiative (SDI) or possibly to complement deterrence, the general consensus in Moscow stands opposed to the development and deployment of space-based defenses.

According to traditional Soviet strategic logic, a U.S. nuclear attack on the Soviet Union is most effectively deterred by keeping U.S. territory vulnerable to retaliation.[1] The "inevitability of mutual destruction," Lev Semeyko of the USA Institute explains, renders nuclear war suicidal for its initiator. Nuclear parity strengthens mutual vulnerability and thereby enhances strategic stability. A decrease in U.S. susceptibility to Soviet retaliation, for instance, as a result of the introduction of weapons in space, would raise the risks of U.S. employment of nuclear arms.[2]

Decisions by the Brezhnev leadership reflected its commitment to sustaining a position of assured mutual destruction. In 1981, it acknowledged that nuclear war cannot be won because retaliation is inescapable,[3] and renounced its first-strike doctrine.[4] The Soviet deterrent since then has rested on a second-strike capability.

Defense Minister Yazov enunciates the Soviet concept of nuclear deterrence in language endorsed by military and civilian strategists alike. He declares that Soviet strategic forces must prevent "an unpunished nuclear attack under any, even the most unfavorable, conditions." The very capacity to retaliate deters aggression against the USSR.[5] The ability to launch a second strike is ensured by rendering Soviet nuclear weapons survivable. Army General Maksimov, the commander-in-chief of the Strategic Missile Forces, singles out "invulnerability" as one of the main requirements for ICBMs.[6] Civilian experts agree that the credibility of deterrence rests on the survivability of the Soviet arsenal.

Strategic parity is supported by many Soviet officials as a way to ensure U.S. vulnerability to retaliation. Even the experts who consider parity unnecessary stress that the Soviet arsenal must be large enough to inflict unacceptable damage on the United States. Soviet strategists see the greatest danger to stability arising from American efforts to threaten or devalue Soviet retaliatory forces. They express grave concern about arms systems, such as the MX and Trident II,[7] and improvements in weapons technology, particularly increased accuracy of U.S. missile warheads and the development of "stealth" technology, which enhance the U.S. potential to destroy Soviet military assets.[8]

Similarly, Soviet experts fear that the introduction of space-based defenses would weaken the Soviet capacity to retaliate against a U.S. nuclear attack. They portray the Strategic Defense Initiative (SDI) as an effort to regain superiority or at least to alter the nuclear balance.[9] The deployment of effective ballistic missile defense (BMD) systems would diminish American vulnerability and thereby reduce Soviet strategic gains. Soviet authorities therefore sought to place the greatest possible restrictions on the SDI program and to ban the development and deployment of weapons in space.

Soviet military officials reacted to SDI initially by threatening to respond with both offensive and defensive systems,[10] but once countermeasures were judged to be cheaper and more effective than ABM systems, they announced their intention of opposing any deployment of SDI solely with offensive arms. American defenses could be saturated by a buildup of missile forces, including decoy ICBMs, or be eluded by radar-reflecting weapons and cruise missiles. An entire BMD system could be crippled by damaging its battle management structure. Soviet scientists concluded that the creation of an impenetrable antiballistic missile shield was impossible and that countermeasures were significantly cheaper than an ABM system itself.[11] Thus, Soviet negotiators persisted in their attempts to retain some link between offensive and defensive weapons. Although they agreed to begin strategic arms cuts without a formal American commitment to abide by the ABM Treaty, they served notice that the emplacement of weapons in space would jeopardize the future of nuclear disarmament.

Interest in ballistic missile defenses can be found in some Soviet quarters. While abiding loosely by the ABM Treaty, the USSR has continued to modernize its strategic defenses, presumably because a small section of the armed forces considers BMD useful in limiting damage if war breaks out. For example, at the end of the 1980s it completed a program to upgrade the world's only operational ABM system, located around Moscow, by replacing above-ground launchers with silo-based ones and deploying new nuclear-armed Gazelle missiles.[12] The Soviet Union has also conducted research into advanced technologies applicable to BMD and space weaponry, but mainly as a hedge against American technological breakthroughs that could lead to the introduction of a large-scale ABM system.[13]

Certain civilian strategists mention the possibility of allowing the deployment of small ABM defenses to strengthen deterrence. Alexei Arbatov suggests that after minimum deterrence is achieved, an antiballistic missile system could be created within the confines of the ABM Treaty to cover only the deployment zones of mobile ICBMs.[14] Even though the proposed system would be too limited to protect most military assets and population centers, it incurred criticism from a military officer for threatening to undermine stability.[15] Arbatov conceives of small-scale defenses as a possible means to enhance stability by reinforcing the survivability of retaliatory forces following deep reductions in strategic arms.

The few Soviet experts who contemplate a shift to BMD have no intention of undermining the USSR's retaliatory potential or of weakening stability. There is little indication that they favor deployment of weapons in space, and they foresee any move to modify the ABM Treaty as a negotiated process that averts a race in defensive arms. A competition in ABM and offensive countermeasures would impose a heavy burden on the Soviet economy, which is already cutting military expenditures it can ill afford and would aggravate tensions between the superpowers, reversing the progress made toward establishing cooperative relations with the United States that facilitate domestic reform.

COMPETING STRATEGIES

With the formal declaration of a no-first-use policy in June 1982, the Soviet Union renounced nuclear preemption and embraced a second-strike doctrine. It undertook efforts to enhance its retaliatory capabilities by increasing the survivability of its nuclear forces. The Gorbachev leadership envisaged further revision in Soviet nuclear strategy and granted civilian strategists the authority to reexamine Soviet requirements for deterrence. The civilians challenged the military to alter its plans for carrying out a second strike. The armed forces appear determined to preserve some counterforce potential in order to retain their strategy of employing nuclear weapons to destroy enemy military targets. Civilian specialists advocate a shift to countervalue targeting, to a strategy of retaliation only against industrial and population centers.

The present reliance on counterforce capability creates some discrepancy between the "sociopolitical" and the "military-technical" aspects of Soviet doctrine or, simply, between nuclear doctrine and strategy. The General Staff rejects the possibility of winning a nuclear war and makes every effort to avert it, but at the same time, must prepare for that eventuality. Nuclear war might break out, and if it does, the Soviet armed forces must be prepared to fight. In fact, they are trained to attack the enemy's strategic arms in an attempt to limit the damage to Soviet territory. Operating under the constraints of the Soviet commitment not to use nuclear weapons first, they would strike second. Resort to preemption is ruled out by government policy, and the political leadership alone has the authority to sanction use of nuclear arms. Nonetheless, Soviet nuclear strategy stresses the need to maintain an effective counterforce capability and a capacity to react swiftly to surprise attack.

The military strategist Mikhail Kiryan explains that strategic operations, which are designed to rout the enemy's strategic groupings, can be carried out either with or without nuclear weapons.[16] The most important objective in war, especially nuclear war, is to limit damage to the Soviet Union by neutralizing the enemy's nuclear potential. The primary military mission in both offense and defense, Kiryan asserts, consists of destroying the opponent's means of nuclear attack. The introduction of nuclear arms, he continues, influences the choice of direction of the main assault, raising the possibility of striking the first blow against enemy nuclear forces.[17] In such an operation, speed is essential. Kiryan argues that the presence of nuclear weapons allows, from the very beginning of war, the achievement of results that can have a deciding impact on the course and even the outcome of war.[18]

Declarations by Defense Minister Yazov appear to confirm Kiryan's assertions that Soviet nuclear weapons would be employed against Western strategic forces, particularly against nuclear arms. Yazov promises that if the Warsaw Pact countries are attacked, "they will give the aggressor a shattering rebuff." Soviet readiness to administer this rebuff, he adds, is related to the fact that NATO reserves the right to use nuclear weapons first and continues to increase its strategic offensive potential.[19] So, even if attacked with nuclear weapons, the Soviet Union will attempt to render the enemy militarily powerless. Yazov stresses that Soviet nuclear forces "from the very beginning of war must be prepared to strike the aggressor and to carry out military missions."[20] These statements appear to confirm the military's intention of responding to a nuclear onslaught by launching weapons against enemy strategic arms in order to cripple the enemy's armed forces and thereby to prevent further losses to the Soviet Union.

Civilian experts demand revision of Soviet nuclear strategy. They urge a reconsideration of the thesis of a "crushing repulse."[21] Alluding to the discrepancy between the second-strike doctrine and the counterforce strategy, Alexei Arbatov castigates Soviet military strategy and tactics for their offensive character and advocates their reorientation in line with the new defensive doctrine.[22] He also points out the danger of relying on launch-on-warning, making clear that his criticism is directed at the Soviet military. [23]

Civilian strategists oppose the General Staff's plans to limit damage in a nuclear war by destroying Western military assets. Arbatov rejects the possibility of keeping losses down to an acceptable level and criticizes Soviet reliance on counterforce targeting. He argues that the potential to eliminate enemy strategic arms fails to correspond to the retaliatory strike doctrine because U.S. missiles will have left their silos by the time the Soviet second strike arrives.[24] Arbatov rules out any employment of Soviet nuclear weapons against the enemy's military might and instead advocates the adoption of a purely countervalue deterrent. "The combat task of offensive and defensive strategic forces will be not to limit damage in the event of nuclear war (which is impossible in any circumstances) nor to defeat the aggressor's armed forces, but to deliver a crushing blow against its life centers." He believes that "targets suitable for retaliation are the aggressor's economic facilities."[25]

Instead of shaping Soviet nuclear forces to destroy U.S. strategic weapons, civilian experts want to restructure the Soviet arsenal in a way that enhances strategic stability and thereby lowers the risk of nuclear war. They argue that the chief factor preventing nuclear war is stability, which, in concrete terms, means reducing the likelihood of a first strike being launched in a crisis situation.[26] In order to minimize the probability of nuclear war, the incentive to strike first must be removed by maintaining a guaranteed retaliatory capability. Strategic stability rests on the threat of inflicting unacceptable damage on an aggressor in response to nuclear attack.[27] Andrei Kokoshin, deputy director of the USA Institute, lays out the military conditions for stability. The strategic environment must remove (1) the stimulus to use nuclear weapons first, (2) the capacity to launch a disarming first strike, and (3) conditions for unsanctioned or accidental nuclear use.[28]

Arbatov notes that striking first confers considerable advantage to one belligerent over the other.[29] The attacker benefits from surprise and from selecting the point of assault. He enjoys much greater chance of success. Even countries harboring no aggressive designs may encounter situations that encourage preemptive attack. They would feel the stimulus to strike first if nuclear attack by the other side seemed impending or if the difference in losses they would suffer from striking first rather than second is great.[30] Ensuring strategic stability requires that the military incentives to strike first be removed. Nuclear strategy should reduce the importance of surprise. While desirable from a strictly military standpoint, Kokoshin argues, a capacity for surprise attack is destabilizing.[31]

A stable balance of nuclear forces provides the main deterrent against a first strike. The chance of success of a preemptive nuclear attack can be eliminated by deploying survivable retaliatory forces. The stimulus to strike first can also be lessened by lowering the ratio of multiple independently targeted reentry vehicles (MIRVs) to missiles. Civilian strategists argue strenuously in favor of deMIRVing. Reducing the ratio of warheads to enemy targets counteracts the dangerous effects of accurate weapons by removing the advantage of attacking and thus decreases the incentive to strike first.[32] The optimal nuclear arsenal, most new thinkers believe, would be composed entirely of single warhead missiles.

Civilian strategists hope to decrease the risks of accidental outbreak of nuclear war by strengthening systems of command, control, and communication (C^3). They see a threat of unsanctioned nuclear use arising from weaknesses in control links.[33] In order to prevent the unauthorized employment of nuclear weapons, they assert, secure C^3 systems must be maintained. Alexei Arbatov indicates a strong preference for two-way lines of communication that are redundant.[34] He observes that the growing complexity of nuclear arms, and of the missions they are assigned, increases the complexity required of C^3 systems. This, in turn, complicates efforts to make C^3 systems survivable, which engenders instability.[35] Deep arms reductions would simplify the tasks of C^3, rendering systems of command and control more secure and thereby reducing the risks of unsanctioned nuclear use.

The military's adherence to a counterforce strategy generates resistance to radical nuclear disarmament. This resistance will grow as the level of weapons falls, because the smaller the size of the Soviet nuclear arsenal, the less adequate potential it offers to destroy enemy military targets. The START accord permits the Soviet Union to keep most of its counterforce strategy intact. Disarmament measures after START would begin to erode the USSR's counterforce potential. Seventy-five percent cuts, by the calculation of Soviet scientists, would leave enough weapons to knock out a wide array of military targets,[36] but beyond that, arms reductions would seriously undermine Soviet counterforce capabilities. Cuts of 95 percent would remove this capability entirely.

FORCE STRUCTURES

The Soviet shift to a second-strike doctrine encouraged the USSR to deploy survivable systems and to create a balanced nuclear triad. The Soviet Union introduced mobile intercontinental ballistic missiles (ICBMs), improved its submarine force, and upgraded the capacity of its strategic aviation. It reduced reliance on ICBMs in favor of nuclear bombers. In line with the military's strategic requirements, modernization programs enhanced Soviet counterforce capabilities. Civilian experts want to restructure Soviet forces to strengthen stability, most notably by curbing warhead proliferation.

In the second half of the 1980s, the fifth generation of Soviet ICBMs was ready for operation. Unlike the SS-17, SS-18, and SS-19, the new missiles were mobile and thus survivable. Deployment of the single warhead SS-25, mounted on a roadworthy launcher, began in 1986. The following year, the SS-24, fitted with ten multiple independently targeted reentry vehicles and transportable by rail, entered service. ICBMs traditionally formed the mainstay of the Soviet deterrent, but from the mid-1980s, the military leadership placed increasing emphasis on sea- and air-based forces. The Strategic Missile Force lost its privileged position among the services, and from 1986, Defense Ministry officials began describing the Soviet nuclear arsenal as a triad.[37]

The buildup of the sea leg of the triad proceeded at a steady pace. The Typhoon class nuclear-powered ballistic missile submarine (SSBN), carrying 20 SS-N-20 missiles with 10 warheads each, entered service in 1982. Delta IV class SSBNs, loaded with 64 MIRVs on top of 16 SS-N-23s, were first deployed in 1985 and were produced at a rate of about one a year. In 1988, SS-N-21 sea-launched cruise missiles (SLCMs) were fitted into Yankee class submarines. The supersonic SS-NX-24 SLCM was undergoing trials at the end of the decade. Improvements in the accuracy of submarine-launched ballistic missiles (SLBMs) developed their capacity to destroy hardened military targets. Modernization of sea-based forces also contributed to the survivability of the Soviet arsenal. The location of Soviet ports allows the U.S. navy in wartime to impede the access of Soviet vessels to the open seas but permits the deployment of Soviet submarines in defensive bastions. Keeping submarines close to Soviet shores, cordoning off sections of the northern seas, and blocking the entry of enemy ships ensures that Soviet submarines can roam home waters in relative safety.

The Soviet high command used to place the least stock in long-range bombers, which, unlike ballistic missiles, were slow in reaching U.S. territory and were liable to interception. In recent years, however, the USSR elevated the status of its strategic bomber forces as the appearance of air-launched cruise missiles (ALCMs) provided Soviet planes with the capacity to hit targets at long range without entering U.S. airspace. In 1984, the Bear H bomber, loaded with AS-15 ALCMs, became operational. The Blackjack bomber, which also carries AS-15s, entered service in 1988. These planes have been assigned to missions and have trained, in an unprecedented step, against the continental United States, thereby reversing the previous policy of using ICBMs for strategic missions and relegating aviation to theater use.[38] Strategic aviation offers greater flexibility than the other two legs of the triad. Bombers can leave their air strips while under attack, give the leadership time to decide whether or not to retaliate, and if necessary be recalled. This flexibility helps to reconcile the second-strike doctrine with the counterforce strategy.

The military leadership strives to establish a more balanced nuclear triad that enhances both survivability and counterforce potential, and to match major new U.S. weapon programs. It is reducing its heavy reliance on ICBMs and diversifying its nuclear forces, in particular by upgrading strategic aviation, to decrease the vulnerability of the Soviet retaliatory potential. Soviet force modernization has improved counterforce capabilities by promoting warhead proliferation. On all three legs of the triad, the number of warheads has increased while the quantity of delivery vehicles has remained static. The USSR has endeavored to duplicate the most significant American introductions of arms systems—sea- and air-launched cruise missiles.

Civilian experts show little interest in increasing the diversity of the Soviet nuclear stockpile. Rather, they select weapon systems that best fulfill the criteria of strategic stability. They criticize deployments of cruise missiles whose accuracy and ability to elude radar detection threaten Soviet retaliatory forces and command centers.[39] They oppose the buildup of air-based forces. Kokoshin expresses concern about bomber survivability, noting that aircraft can be destroyed on the ground by enemy conventional arms.[40] Arbatov argues that ballistic missiles can hit most of the important targets, so there is no need for heavy bombers. Elimination of strategic aviation would remove the USSR's justification for maintaining large and costly air defenses.[41]

Civilian strategists favor ballistic missile systems, such as SS-25 ICBMs and SS-N-23 missiles on Delta IV submarines, which are placed in survivable launchers and loaded with a minimum of warheads.[42] However, they are divided over the appropriate mix of land- and sea-based forces. Some regard SLBMs as the most effective instrument of retaliation[43] and recommend the emplacement of the entire Soviet nuclear arsenal on board submarines.[44] Others consider sea-based nuclear weapons unstable. The problems of communicating with submarines can render tight control over them difficult to exercise, which increases the possibility of unsanctioned nuclear use.[45] The survivability of Soviet submarines is placed at risk by the U.S. forward maritime strategy and anti-submarine warfare capabilities. The Soviet Union, they believe, ought to avoid competition in sea-based forces in which the United States enjoys technological and geographic advantages.[46] Some civilian strategists suggest that the Soviet arsenal should be composed of a combination of submarines and mobile ICBMs,[47] perhaps with SLBMs carrying single warheads.[48] Others argue that the optimal minimum deterrence would consist entirely of light mobile ICBMs.[49]

Disagreements among civilians over basing modes for ballistic missiles can complicate radical nuclear disarmament. The main impediment to deep arms cuts is the difference in force requirements set by the General Staff and the civilian strategists. The Soviet high command wants to enhance stability[50] but is reluctant to give up the Soviet capacity to destroy enemy nuclear forces.

It shares neither the great enthusiasm of civilians for deMIRVing nor their interest in complete reliance on ballistic missiles. As the size of the Soviet nuclear arsenal diminishes, disagreements over its composition will grow more pronounced. Kokoshin argues that the lower the level of armaments, the more stringently the criteria for stability need to be applied.[51] As cuts get deeper, civilian strategists will insist all the more strenuously on retaining their preferred nuclear weapons and weakening the Soviet counterforce potential.

Force structures will be shaped increasingly in the future by the need to conclude accords with the United States. Zhurkin observes that the process of disarmament tends to make the nuclear arsenals of the two sides more symmetrical, increasingly so as arms reductions proceed further. Lowering the level of weapons constrains the freedom of the sides to choose the composition of their nuclear forces.[52] Concluding accords after START, in the view of Arbatov, requires Soviet-American understanding on the principles of stability and virtually joint regulation of the strategic balance.[53] The preference of new thinkers to avoid emulating Western arms programs makes them inclined to field different weapons with commensurate capabilities, but agreement with the United States on deep arms cuts would be easier to reach if the sides retained analogous weapon systems.

WEAPONS IN EUROPE

Gorbachev and his supporters embarked on nuclear disarmament in order to strengthen military stability in Europe. They believed that NATO's resort to nuclear weapons could be prevented more effectively by removing U.S. arms from the continent than by building up a favorable alignment of theater nuclear forces. In the early 1980s, the Soviet Union planned to deter escalation of a conventional conflict to a nuclear war by enhancing its nuclear potential, in particular by deploying SS-20s. However, the introduction of Pershing-2 and cruise missiles undercut Soviet attempts to establish parity at the theater-strategic level and persuaded the Soviet government to eliminate intermediate-range missiles (IRMs). The Gorbachev leadership reached the conclusion that Soviet preponderance in short-range and tactical systems was insufficient to avert escalation. Scrapping short-range missiles (SRMs) and reducing tactical nuclear weapons (TNWs) served to decrease further the risk of nuclear war.

A brief summary of the labels used to denote weapon systems and arms talks should help to clarify the issues. Some of these terms differ from those commonly accepted but more accurately describe what was being negotiated. The talks on nuclear weapons in Europe are usually referred to as the Intermediate-range Nuclear Forces (INF) negotiations. This name was appropriate until 1985 but later became a misnomer. The USSR, in October 1985, agreed to shift discussion of intermediate-range aircraft to the strategic arms reduction talks. In January 1986, the Soviet Union dropped its insistence on counting British and French nuclear forces (which are deployed on land, air, and sea). From then on, the talks covered only missiles. Intermediate-range missiles constituted the main topic of negotiations, but short-range missiles were also discussed and were subsequently integrated formally into the talks and included in the treaty signed at the Washington summit in December 1987. Thus, the treaty bears the name Intermediate- and Shorter-Range Missiles (ISRM). Herein, the negotiations are referred to as INF for the period 1981-1985 and as ISRM for the years 1986-1987.

Theater nuclear forces in Europe can be divided into three categories: intermediate-range (1,000 to 5,500 km), short-range (500 to 1,000 km), and tactical (less than 500 km). The "zero option," or first zero, involved intermediate-range missiles; Soviet SS-4s, SS-5s, and SS-20s; U.S. Pershing-2s; and ground-launched cruise missiles (GLCMs) on both sides. The second zero encompassed short-range missiles, the USSR's SS-12/22s and SS-23s, and the Pershing-1s of the United States. The double zero established by the ISRM Treaty covered these two categories of weapons. The Soviet Union foresees the achievement of a third zero, which would eliminate tactical nuclear weapons (TNWs), including missiles, artillery, and aircraft.

By the late 1970s, Soviet military planners decided that they could achieve strategic objectives in the European theater without resort to nuclear arms and that their overriding aim was to restrain the threat of the enemy's nuclear use. The USSR developed operational concepts and combat capabilities to inhibit NATO's employment of nuclear forces and to reduce the impact of any nuclear weapons that might be launched.[54] Soviet strategists preferred, in the event of hostilities, to conduct military missions using only conventional arms. First Deputy Chief of the General Staff Gareyev revised previous estimates that a major conventional conflict would probably escalate after a certain period into nuclear exchanges and envisaged the possibility of waging a relatively long war solely with conventional weapons.[55] This possibility could be increased by deterring NATO's resort to nuclear arms.

The presence of nuclear weapons enhanced the Soviet Union's combat potential and thereby discouraged both conventional and nuclear attack. Soviet military strategists prepared to fight a war in Europe either with or without nuclear forces. If nuclear arms were introduced, the USSR would carry out combined-arms operations in which nuclear weapons, integrated into general purpose forces, would strengthen the Soviet capacity to rout enemy formations. Destruction of Western nuclear weapons would represent a primary strategic objective.[56] While hostilities remained at the conventional level, enemy nuclear missiles could be knocked out preemptively by Soviet conventional arms.[57] Soviet nuclear assets would remain in reserve to retaliate against a nuclear strike.

The Soviet Union in the late 1970s and early 1980s augmented its theater nuclear potential to reinforce deterrence in Europe. The USSR introduced the SS-20 mobile IRM with three accurate warheads, SS-12/22 and SS-23 SRMs, and the SS-21 tactical missile. Nuclear capable artillery was modernized, new versions of tactical aircraft were produced and deployment of medium-range Backfire bombers continued apace. During this period, Soviet procurement priorities gave precedence to theater over strategic nuclear weapons. Soviet officials now admit that the USSR acquired the capacity to wage a limited nuclear war in Europe.[58]

The SS-20 missile was intended to boost the USSR's capability to deter NATO employment of nuclear arms. The Soviet Union deployed SS-20s to offset U.S. forward-based systems and British and French nuclear forces, to achieve nuclear parity at the theater-strategic level, and to weaken NATO's ability to control escalation in a European war. However, these Soviet gains were undermined by the introduction of Pershing-2 and ground-launched cruise missiles (GLCMs). The Pershing-2 ballistic missile could hit a target on Soviet territory with considerable accuracy in about one-third of the time of an ICBM fired from the United States. Vitali Zhurkin, drawing an analogy to the German invasion of World War II, remarked that the location and speed of Pershing-2s meant that "the nuclear threat was found literally at the gates of Moscow."[59] Soviet observers considered Tomahawk GLCMs less alarming but still a matter of grave concern. The subsonic speed of Tomahawks extended their flight time to two or three hours, but their virtual invisibility to ground radars provided them with good opportunities to reach the USSR undetected and to destroy Soviet military assets.

The emplacement of Pershing-2 and GLCMs in Western Europe reinforced NATO's capacity to dominate escalation and to confine a nuclear war to Europe. The U.S. missiles could knock out important military targets, including Soviet nuclear forces and command centers, and inflict heavy damage on the USSR, while the U.S. strategic arsenal remained intact and in a position to devastate the Soviet homeland. Since Tomahawk and Pershing-2 missiles significantly increased the likelihood of NATO's resort to nuclear weapons in the event of war in Europe, the Soviet Union was willing to pay a high price to get rid of them.

The military benefits derived from eliminating short-range and tactical nuclear arms were less apparent. Intermediate-range missiles could place the USSR at the great disadvantage of waging a war that affected the most industrially advanced and agriculturally fertile part of its country and left the United States unscathed. In contrast, SRMs and TNWs could be employed in a theater war, limited for the Soviet Union as well as the United States, which encompassed only central Europe. Nuclear arms provide defending troops with the capacity to thwart an enemy's ground attack.[60] They decrease the possibility of a Western invasion while the USSR is scaling down dramatically its military presence in Eastern Europe. Retaining some tactical nuclear weapons compensates for the Soviet Union asymmetrical cuts in conventional forces.[61]

The Gorbachev leadership has pursued the elimination of SRMs and the reduction of TNWs to enhance military stability on the continent by lowering the risk of escalation of conventional to nuclear war and strengthening the defensive elements of force postures. Soviet experts are skeptical of the USSR's ability to dissuade NATO from taking recourse to nuclear weapons. They regard a planned nuclear attack as a remote possibility, but express concern about conventional hostilities expanding into a nuclear conflict.[62] A conventional war, in their judgment, can escalate at any time, especially in a crisis situation.[63] Both civilian and military strategists expect the losing side in a conventional conflict to introduce nuclear arms rather than accept defeat.[64]

The existing operational plans and capabilities to fight a nuclear war limited to central Europe are considered by many, especially civilian, experts to be destabilizing. The integration of tactical nuclear weapons into general purpose forces creates a high probability of nuclear use.[65] Employment of conventional strikes to destroy enemy nuclear assets generates a great risk of enemy retaliation with nuclear weapons.[66] The ample chance of escalation to the nuclear level, which results in part from the USSR's own military preparations, provides a strong incentive to remove nuclear forces from Europe.

Civilian analysts argue that TNWs enhance each side's capacity for attack. Nuclear arms confer a great military advantage when used for offensive aims. Chief of the Ground Forces' Political Directorate Popkov notes that the USSR is prepared to exploit the results of Soviet nuclear strikes by bringing up reserves and launching an in-depth assault at high speed.[67] In contrast, the role of TNWs in defensive operations has yet to be thought through by the Soviet high command.[68] Thus, reduction of tactical nuclear weapons serves to limit offensive capabilities.

The USSR prosecutes negotiations on Conventional Forces in Europe (CFE) to constrain the capacity of either alliance to invade the other. By removing the possibility to launch a surprise attack and decreasing the ability to conduct large-scale offensive operations, conventional arms cuts can create a more stable military balance and raise the nuclear threshold.[69] Elimination of the potential to defeat an enemy militarily greatly lessens the danger of nuclear use. At the same time, lowering the level of TNWs stimulates conventional force cuts. The military leadership considered Soviet conventional superiority necessary to offset NATO's nuclear advantages.[70] It is wary of giving up preponderance in tanks and manpower without substantial reductions in tactical nuclear arsenals. Since TNW cuts reinforce the stabilizing effects of removing conventional imbalances and offensive potentials, and some weapon systems have the dual-capability to fire both conventional and nuclear charges,[71] the adoption of defensive force postures requires concomitant progress in CFE and TNW talks.

Soviet civilian strategists propose TNW cuts that promote reductions in conventional arms and that decrease the risk of war by enhancing the ability of both sides to deter attack. Rather than concentrate on preserving equality in numbers or capabilities, they want to strengthen the nuclear balance by maintaining survivable weapon systems with secure command and control links.[72] They are interested in restricting NATO's nuclear modernization program, which would increase the alliance's offensive potential, and in eliminating battlefield nuclear arms to raise the nuclear threshold.[73]

The Gorbachev leadership has embarked on nuclear disarmament to reinforce deterrence by decreasing the capacity of either side to conduct successful military operations using nuclear arms. It sacrifices Soviet advantages in an effort to curb U.S. weapon programs. The USSR attempts to constrain the SDI program that threatens to devalue Soviet retaliatory capabilities. Reductions in first-strike potentials, particularly in heavy ICBMs, are designed to diminish the risks of nuclear attack. Relinquishing Soviet preponderance in intermediate- and short-range missiles has secured the elimination of American Pershing-2s and GLCMs and served to minimize the possibility of conventional hostilities in Europe degenerating into nuclear war. The Soviet Union seeks to restrict the U.S. weapon systems that it deems most threatening, namely those best suited for preemption and those incorporating advanced technologies.

By strengthening the nuclear balance, arms control enhances political stability. Bilateral moves to restructure nuclear arsenals require cooperation and build trust between the superpowers. Disarmament relieves Western pressure on the USSR by limiting American first-strike capabilities and technologically sophisticated U.S. weapons, and thereby renders the Soviet Union secure enough to compromise on a wide range of international issues and to create an opening to the West. Soviet concessions demonstrate the USSR's commitment to stability and stimulate Western interest in establishing cooperative relations.

NOTES

1. Lev S. Semeyko, "SS-20: Oshibka, no Menshaya, chem Mozhno Bylo by Dumat" ["SS-20: A Mistake, but Smaller than Would Be Thought"] *SShA: Ekonomika, Politika, Ideologia*, December 1988, p. 33.
2. Lev Semeyko in *Krasnaya Zvezda*, 23 January 1986.
3. Leonid Brezhnev in *Pravda*, 21 October 1981.
4. Dmitri Ustinov in *Pravda*, 7 November 1981.
5. *Pravda*, 27 July 1987.
6. Interviewed in *New Times*, no. 51 (December), 1986, p. 12.

7. Alexei Arbatov, "Glubokoye Sokrashcheniye Strategicheskykh Vooruzheny" ["Deep Reduction of Strategic Arms"], *Mirovaya Ekonomika i Mezhdunarodnye Otnoshenia (MEMO)*, May 1988, p. 28.
8. Viktor Starodubov in *Pravda*, 27 January 1989.
9. For instance, Makhmut A. Gareyev, *Sovetskaya Voyennaya Nauka* [Soviet Military Science] (Moscow: Znaniye, 1988), p. 8, and Andrei A. Kokoshin and Valentin V. Larionov, *Predotvrashcheniye Voyny: Doktriny, Kontseptsy, Perspektivy* [War Prevention: Doctrines, Concepts, Prospects] (Moscow: Progress, 1990), p. 47.
10. Sergei Akhromeyev in *Pravda*, 19 October 1985.
11. Yevgeni Velikhov, Roald Sagdeyev, and Andrei Kokoshin (eds.), *Weaponry in Space: The Dilemma of Security* (Moscow: Mir, 1986), pp. 98–104.
12. Thomas B. Cochran, William M. Arkin, Robert S. Norris, and Jeffrey I. Sands, *Nuclear Weapons Databook: Volume 4, Soviet Nuclear Weapons* (New York: Harper & Row, 1989), pp. 116–17.
13. Bruce Parrott, *The Soviet Union and Ballistic Missile Defense* (Boulder, CO: Westview, 1987), p. 82.
14. Yevgeni Primakov (ed.), *IMEMO Disarmament and Security Yearbook 1987* (Moscow: Novosti, 1988), pp. 83–84.
15. Maj. Gen. Yu. Lyubimov, "O Dostatochnosti Oborony i Nedostatke Kompetentnosti" ["On Defense Suffiency and Inadequacy of Competence"], *Kommunist Vooruzhennykh Sil*, no. 16 (August), 1989, p. 26.
16. Lt. Gen. Mikhail M. Kiryan, *Istoria Voyennovo Iskusstva* [*The History of Military Art*] (Moscow: Voyenizdat, 1986), pp. 408, 410.
17. Ibid., p. 414.
18. Ibid., p. 407.
19. *Pravda*, 27 July 1987.
20. Dmitri T. Yazov, *Na Strazhe Sotsializma i Mira*, [*On Guard for Socialism and Peace*] (Moscow: Voyenizdat, 1987), p. 40.
21. Yuli Vorontsov, "Military-Political Aspects of Security," *International Affairs*, October 1988, p. 41.
22. *IMEMO Yearbook 1987*, pp. 210–12.
23. Ibid., pp. 271–75.
24. Ibid., p. 213.
25. Alexei Arbatov, "How Much Defense is Sufficient?" *International Affairs*, April 1989, pp. 34–36.
26. Alexei Arbatov, "Glubokoye Sokrashcheniye Strategicheskykh Vooruzhennykh," p. 21.
27. Andrei Kokoshin, "Razvitiye Voyennovo Dela i Sokrashcheniye Vooruzhennykh Sil i Obychnykh Vooruzheny" ["The Evolution of Military Affairs and the Reduction of Armed Forces and Conventional Armaments"], *MEMO*, January 1988, p. 29.

28. Andrei Kokoshin, "Sokrashcheniye Yadernykh Vooruzhennykh i Strategicheskaya Stabilnost" ["Reduction of Nuclear Arms and Strategic Stability"], *SShA*, February 1988, p. 4.
29. *IMEMO Yearbook 1987*, pp. 217-18.
30. Arbatov, "Glubokoye Sokrashcheniye Strategicheskykh Vooruzheny," p. 22.
31. Kokoshin, "Razvitiye Voyennovo," p. 28.
32. Kokoshin, "Sokrashcheniye Yadernykh Vooruzheny," p. 9.
33. Yuri Ya. Kirshin, "Politika i Voyennaya Strategia v Yaderny Vek" ["Politics and Military Strategy in the Nuclear Age"], *MEMO*, November 1988, pp. 41-42.
34. *IMEMO Yearbook 1987*, p. 267.
35. Ibid., p. 270.
36. Kokoshin, "Sokrashcheniye Yadernykh Vooruzheny," p. 6.
37. Vitali Shabanov in *Krasnaya Zvezda*, 15 August 1986, quoted in Rose E. Gottemoeller, *Conflict and Consensus in the Soviet Armed Forces* (Santa Monica, CA: RAND, October 1989), p. 29.
38. Rose E. Gottemoeller, *Land-attack Cruise Missiles*, Adelphi Paper no. 226 (London: IISS, Winter 1987/88), p. 11.
39. Arbatov, "Glubokoye Sokrashcheniye Strategicheskykh Vooruzheny," p. 24.
40. Kokoshin, "Sokrashcheniye Yadernykh Vooruzheny," p. 9.
41. Arbatov, "How Much Defense is Sufficient?" p. 38.
42. Radomir Bogdanov and Andrei Kortunov, "On the Balance of Power," *International Affairs*, August 1989, p. 8.
43. Genrikh Trofimenko, "Towards a New Quality in Soviet-American Relations," *International Affairs*, December 1988, p. 21.
44. Sergei Vybornov, Andrei Gusenkov, and Vladimir Leontiev, "Nothing Is Simple in Europe," *International Affairs*, March 1988, p. 40.
45. Kokoshin, "Sokrashcheniye Yadernykh Vooruzheny," pp. 6, 9.
46. Vitali V. Zhurkin, Sergei A. Karaganov, and Andrei V. Kortunov, "O Razumnoy Dostatotchnosti," ["On Reasonable Sufficiency"], *SShA*, December 1987, p. 17.
47. Bogdanov and Kortunov, "On the Balance of Power," p. 8.
48. Ednan Agayev, "Towards a New Model of Strategic Stability," *International Affairs*, March 1989, p. 101.
49. Kokoshin, "Sokrashcheniye Yadernykh Vooruzheny," p. 9.
50. Dmitri T. Yazov, "Novaya Model Bezopasnosti i Vooruzhennye Sily" ["A New Model of Security and the Armed Forces"], *Kommunist*, no. 18 (December), 1989, p. 65, and Moiseyev in *Krasnaya Zvezda*, 7 July 1990.
51. Ibid., p. 6.
52. Zhurkin, Karaganov, and Kortunov, "O Razumnoy Dostatotchnosti," p. 17.

53. Alexei Arbatov, "New Military Thinking in East and West," *New Times*, no. 1 (January), 1990, p. 25.
54. Phillip A. Petersen and Notra Trulock III, "Soviet Views and Policies towards Theater War in Europe," in Robbin F. Laird and Susan B. Clark (eds.), *The USSR and the Western Alliance* (Boston: Unwin Hyman, 1990), p. 26.
55. Col. Gen. Makhmut A. Gareyev, *M. V. Frunze—Voyenny Teoretik* [*M. V. Frunze—Military Theorist*] (Moscow: Voyenizdat, 1985), p. 240.
56. Kiryan, *Istoria Voyennovo Iskusstva*, pp. 411-16.
57. Gareyev, *M. V. Frunze*, p. 245.
58. Sergei V. Kortunov, "Vozmozhny li Peregovory po Takticheskomu Yadernomu Oruzhiyu?" ["Are Negotiations on Tactical Nuclear Weapons Possible?"], *MEMO*, February 1990, pp. 30-31.
59. Vitali V. Zhurkin, Sergei A. Karaganov and Andrei V. Kortunov, "Vyzovy Bezopasnosti—Starye i Novye" ["Challenges of Security—Old and New"], *Kommunist*, no. 1 (January), 1988, p. 44.
60. Kiryan, *Istoria Voyennovo Iskusstva*, p. 416.
61. Pavel Bayev, Vitali Zhurkin, Sergei Karaganov, and Viktor Shein, *Tactical Nuclear Weapons in Europe* (Moscow: Novosti, 1990), p. 13.
62. Aleksandr Ye. Bovin and Vladimir P. Lukin, "Na Poroge Novovo Veka" ["At the Threshold of the New Century"], *MEMO*, December 1987, p. 61.
63. Yazov, *Na Strazhe Sotsializma i Mira*, p. 31.
64. Arbatov in *IMEMO Yearbook 1987*, p. 215 and Gareyev, *Sovetskaya Voyennaya Nauka*, p. 7.
65. Vladimir Baranovsky in *IMEMO Yearbook 1987*, p. 55.
66. Vitali Shabanov, " 'Conventional' Warfare: New Dangers," *New Times*, no. 46 (November), 1986, p. 8 and Andrei A. Kokoshin and Valentin V. Larionov, "Protivostoyanniye Sil Obshchevo Naznachenia v Kontekste Obespechenia Strategicheskoy Stabilnosti" ["The Balance of Conventional Forces in the Context of Ensuring Strategic Stability"], *MEMO*, June 1988, p. 28.
67. Quoted in Aleksandr G. Savelyev, "Predotvrashcheniye Voyny i Sderzhivaniye: Podkhody OVD i NATO" ["War Prevention and Deterrence: The Approaches of WTO and NATO"], *MEMO*, June 1989, p. 25.
68. Bayev et al., *Tactical Nuclear Weapons in Europe*, pp. 39-40.
69. Andrei Kokoshin, Alexander Konovalov, Valentin Larionov, and Valeri Mazing, *Problems of Ensuring Stability with Radical Cuts in Armed Forces and Conventional Armaments in Europe* (Moscow: Novosti, 1989), pp. 5-6.
70. Bayev et al., *Tactical Nuclear Weapons in Europe*, pp. 10, 38.

71. Valentin V. Larionov, "Problemy Predotvrashchenia Obychnnoy Voyny v Evrope" ["Problems of Preventing Conventional War in Europe"], *MEMO*, July 1989, pp. 32-33.
72. Bayev et. al., *Tactical Nuclear Weapons in Europe*, pp. 38-39.
73. Ibid., pp. 25-26, 43-44.

5

THE DIPLOMACY OF ARMS CONTROL

Gorbachev and his advisors seek genuine cooperation with the West leading to full Soviet participation in the international system. They have therefore scaled down Soviet defense capabilities, imparted flexibility to Soviet foreign policy, made concessions to accommodate Western interests, and accepted Western modes of interaction. Substantial cuts in, and restructuring of, nuclear arsenals minimize the risk of conflict and reduce the threat posed by each side's armed forces to the other. Strengthening the military balance eliminates sources of antagonism and enhances stability in the political sphere.

Arms control develops common interests with the United States and Western Europe and provides evidence of modified Soviet intentions. It removes weapons rivalry from the center of Soviet-American relations and permits expansion of cooperation across the board. In turn, improvement in the overall climate of relations stimulates further progress in disarmament.

Soviet policy appealed to pragmatic Republicans in the United States to reduce reliance on military power. The USSR offered to cut its strategic capabilities to entice influential members of the administration and Congress to curb U.S. force modernization and conclude arms accords. In particular, Soviet concessions were designed to complement the erosion of domestic support for the SDI program and to render more attractive a grand compromise trading cuts in offensive arms for restrictions on the development of defensive systems.

Nuclear disarmament in Europe served to bring down divisions on the continent. Western Europe, according to Soviet observers, was inclined to forge close relations with the USSR but was constrained by the strategic link to the United States. The easing of superpower tensions diminished NATO's need to rest its security on U.S. nuclear guarantees and facilitated nuclear arms reductions, which granted Western Europe the opportunity to replace gradually the alliance systems with new security structures.

REASSESSING PAST POLICY

Gorbachev's accession to the post of general secretary prompted a reevaluation of foreign policy. In an effort to encourage the leadership to alter course, Soviet international affairs experts criticized mistakes and shortcomings evident in the USSR's actions in previous years. They found fault with both the methods and the orientation of Soviet policy toward the West.

Soviet specialists concluded that tactics formerly employed had proved counterproductive. Georgi Sturua of *IMEMO* argued that past foreign policy "lacked a readiness for prudent compromise, flexibility, and drive."[1] In addition to rigidity, Soviet practices had exhibited unnecessary deceptiveness and heavy-handedness. The influential political editor of *Izvestia*, Aleksandr Bovin, remarked that "craftiness" in diplomacy ought to be used in inverse proportion to the importance of the problem under discussion. He also criticized former Soviet leaderships for issuing ultimatums because this limited the government's options, froze its position, and thereby hindered it from correcting policy in response to changes in the situation.[2] The Soviet decision to walk out of the arms talks in November 1983, Soviet commentators acknowledged, had misfired. Breaking off the negotiations had failed to achieve the anticipated impact.[3]

Soviet experts deprecated the unsophisticated analyses of world politics that were commonplace in the Brezhnev period and that have, to some extent, persisted. Deputy Director of *IMEMO* Oleg Bykov expressed his annoyance with "the hackneyed, stereotyped assessments that are still characteristic of some of our commentators" and that offer a "negative depiction of everything related to the official American line" in contrast to "the demonstrators carrying signs." This, he concludes, "is an inadequate reflection of reality."[4] Soviet observers had often failed to distinguish partially sympathetic political groups in the United States, especially in the U.S. government, from completely hostile ones.

Bykov saw the same unimaginative approach pervading Soviet conduct of arms talks. He criticized Soviet negotiators for weighing the strategic balance as if "using an apothecary's scales," for conceiving of disarmament as the reduction "of an absolutely identical number of weapons by both sides," and for demonstrating "unwarranted rigidity" in "understanding how 'trade-offs' in quantity and quality and in other components of the strategic equation can be made with a view to reaching agreements."[5] Soviet arms negotiators were so obsessed by numbers that they neglected qualitative measures of the nuclear balance and lost opportunities to exchange superior numbers on one side for qualitative advantages on the other.

Obstinacy in negotiations, according to Soviet experts, undermined Soviet efforts in the long run. Disarmament deserved to be treated as an urgent necessity because, Bykov explained, negotiations were lagging behind the arms race. The development of military technology was proceeding at an accelerating rate, which increased the difficulty of placing modern armaments under control.[6] Failure to restrain the arms race, he noted, could have grave consequences for strategic stability.[7] Georgi Arbatov, director of the USA Institute, shared Bykov's concern. He was worried about the inability of disarmament negotiations to keep pace with the introduction of new weapon systems, citing as an example the unconstrained proliferation of first-strike weapons.[8] The past Soviet practice of slow and stubborn bargaining, Arbatov argued, left arms talks "doomed to discuss not so much the problems of today and tomorrow as the problems of yesterday." He suggested that more attention be given at the highest level of government to arms limitation and reduction. Negotiations could be accelerated by reaching basic understandings between foreign ministers and then instructing delegations in Geneva to work out the details.[9] In fact, Gorbachev and Shevardnadze addressed arms control as a high-priority issue to ensure rapid progress in disarmament.

According to Soviet international affairs specialists, the Soviet government needed more than sophisticated analyses of world events and flexible diplomacy. The orientation of Soviet foreign policy required fundamental change. New thinking acknowledged the limited utility of military power, the negative impact of Soviet arms buildup on external relations, and the need for closer cooperation with the West. Consequently, the Gorbachev leadership reduced the emphasis on security issues and accorded greater consideration to other aspects of East-West interaction.

IMPROVING SUPERPOWER RELATIONS

Gorbachev and his advisors set out to develop constructive interaction with the United States. They wanted to establish a Soviet-American relationship far more harmonious than that experienced in the 1970s, one that would permit the achievement of nuclear disarmament. Détente, Georgi Sturua explains, was "approached as a zero-sum game." It preserved the confrontation between social systems, so it naturally made Americans skeptical. Since Soviet leaders themselves were affirming that "détente must promote the spread of socialism throughout the world," conservatives in the United States concluded that "there can be no mutually profitable détente since our interests are irreconcilable." Thus, the improvement in U.S.-Soviet relations in the 1970s, Sturua argued, produced agreements that merely regulated the main parameters of the arms race but failed to create the conditions necessary to achieve real disarmament.[10]

In order to promote arms reductions, Gorbachev and his supporters undertook the task of establishing stable and constructive Soviet-American relations. The rapport between the superpowers consists of expanding areas of convergence and fostering a process of the mutual influence that broadens the community of interests. The reorientation of Soviet foreign policy has provided the main impetus for bringing the USSR and the United States closer together. Sturua asserts that Soviet-American relations moved "to a higher level" and gained "a more civilized character" largely as a result of "the revision commenced by the Soviet Union of the approaches and dogmas that predominated in the 1970s and brought about the short-lived nature of détente."[11]

The Gorbachev leadership's policy toward the United States was designed to generate a broad basis for cooperation, in part by lowering the military content of relations. Up to the mid-1980s, resolution of disputes in the military sphere was considered a prerequisite for normal Soviet-American relations. The superpower dialogue centered on arms negotiations and broke down when the INF talks collapsed. In 1984, the USSR refused to resume the arms talks unless the United States withdrew its newly emplaced missiles from Western Europe. The Soviet leadership later dropped this demand and agreed to reopen the superpower dialogue, but kept arms control as the main focus of relations. The Politburo, after the Geneva summit, issued a reminder that "the determining factor in Soviet-American relations will continue to be the sphere of security, the core of which consists of the problems of preventing the militarization of space and reducing nuclear arms."[12] In 1987, Gorbachev called the arms race the main obstacle to good superpower relations.[13]

Gradually, Soviet policy under Gorbachev elevated the importance of other issues and constructed a wider base for East-West relations. While the first two Reagan-Gorbachev meetings were devoted, at Soviet insistence, almost entirely to discussion of SDI and nuclear weapons, subsequent summits addressed a broader range of questions, including human rights, regional conflicts, and bilateral issues. This reflected Soviet interest in improving the overall climate of superpower relations, which served to facilitate progress in disarmament. Fostering warm relations and reducing nuclear weapons were seen as trends that reinforced each other.[14]

The Gorbachev leadership softened its position on nuclear arms control before compromising on other issues. Soviet concessions on disarmament offered the most immediate way of demonstrating the change in Soviet intentions and testing Western willingness to deal constructively with the USSR. They assuaged Western enmity and thereby alleviated direct military pressure on the Soviet Union, which shored up domestic support for reducing military priorities and resolving Soviet differences with the United States. Progress in arms control facilitated Soviet compromise on the treatment of Soviet dissidents and on disputes in the Third World. The overall improvement in Soviet-American relations, in turn, built sufficient trust on both sides to sustain the disarmament process.

The focus of Soviet diplomacy shifted away from military affairs as other issues received growing attention. The USSR made conciliatory gestures on human rights, releasing such prominent dissidents as Andrei Sakharov, and cooperated with the United States in resolving regional conflicts. Regular encounters of Soviet and U.S. officials were established to exchange views on problems arising in various parts of the world. The sides signed agreements leading to the Soviet withdrawal from Afghanistan and to the creation of an independent Namibian state. The Soviet Union strengthened its ties to the United States, expanded scientific and technological cooperation, including peaceful space research, and enlarged trade links, courting potential American investors. These policy changes, aside from their own considerable merits, provided an atmosphere far more conducive to arms control.

As superpower relations grew warmer, dialogue on military issues became less contentious and more constructive. The area of discussion has been enlarged to encompass military doctrines, weapon programs, and defense budgets. Contacts have increased. Yazov's encounter in Switzerland with U.S. Secretary of Defense Carlucci in March 1988 was followed by a series of meetings at the ministerial level and between service chiefs, military experts, and parliamentarians responsible for overseeing the armed forces. Thus, the Soviet leadership began to develop cooperation with the United States in the field of defense.

The USSR was helped in improving Soviet-American relations by changes in the U.S. government. The steady increase in the influence of Republican moderates during Reagan's second term bolstered the prospects for constructive interaction between the superpowers. Already in 1985, Deputy Director of the USA Institute Andrei Kokoshin observed pragmatic elements inside the Reagan administration and the Republican Party trying to gain control over policy making. These elements supported much of the arms buildup but were also firm advocates of arms control. They rejected the possibility of winning a nuclear war and considered military superiority unattainable.[15] The views of Republican moderates on nuclear war and military superiority were endorsed by Reagan in 1985. He was persuaded by Gorbachev at the Geneva summit to issue a joint statement declaring that victory in nuclear war is impossible and pledging not to seek military superiority. Some Soviet officials refused to take Reagan at his word. While Gorbachev and committed proponents of new thinking stopped accusing the United States of trying to achieve military superiority, other members of the Soviet establishment continued to do so for the duration of the Reagan presidency.[16]

During the course of 1986, Soviet experts saw Reagan vacillating between two tendencies in his administration. The U.S. government continued its intense accumulation of military power but was split between right-wing groups that opposed on principle negotiated arms reductions and pragmatists who advocated a constructive dialogue with the Soviet Union. Political forces within the administration appeared quite evenly matched, but the balance was tilting in favor of the moderates. The standing of

Defense Secretary Weinberger diminished slightly, while that of Secretary of State Shultz grew.[17] Despite signs of growing moderation in U.S. policy, some Soviet officials felt uneasy about doing business with Reagan. They still considered him too reactionary to deal with, and they preferred to postpone arms control until Reagan left office. Gorbachev strongly disagreed. He retorted shortly before the Reykjavik summit that the issues facing the superpowers were too pressing "for us simply to decide that we are going to 'stand still' for two and a half years."[18]

In 1987, U.S. policy made a significant departure from the former "confrontational course." Saddled by the huge budget deficit, assaulted by opponents in Congress, and discredited by the Iran-contra affair, right-wing members of the Reagan administration lost much of their influence. The leading proponents of unbridled competition with the Soviet Union, Caspar Weinberger and Richard Perle, left the government. As a result, pragmatists such as George Shultz and Frank Carlucci rose in stature.[19]

Sergei Rogov of the USA Institute argued that traditional Reaganism (espousing military superiority and confrontation) had peaked in 1984, and then the administration shifted gradually to the center (in favor of strategic parity and reduced superpower tensions).[20] The shift was part of a long-term trend. Rogov expected the budgetary constraints that beset Reagan's administration to affect his successor. The United States would find great difficulty initiating a further escalation of the nuclear arms race. The programs launched by Reagan to reequip all three legs of the strategic triad left no room for new supplementary programs. Any additional military efforts would require cuts in other parts of the defense budget.[21]

As Reagan's second term wore on, Soviet specialists on foreign affairs saw the threat posed by the Strategic Defense Initiative recede dramatically. Although they expressed apprehension about military spin-offs from SDI and about the dangerous impact of an introduction of space weapons, they considered SDI a drain on the U.S. economy whose cost would most likely prohibit large-scale development and deployment. Research into exotic technologies held out little chance for successful development of space-based defenses, and domestic support for SDI was eroding. The growing budgetary and political constraints imposed on SDI increased the prospects for the Soviet Union to achieve its primary aim of enhancing strategic stability by preserving the Anti-Ballistic Missile Treaty.

Soviet natural and social scientists were not worried about SDI stimulating economic growth and technological progress in the United States. In fact, their studies indicated that SDI would have the opposite effect.[22] The civilian, rather than the military, sector is the main source of technological advancement. SDI has a negative impact on the U.S. economy by squeezing out civilian research and development, thereby slowing down technological progress and reducing the growth rate of labor productivity.

Most inventions and discoveries, Soviet scientists found, result from civilian research and development. Military research in the United States is a poor source of innovation. Most Defense Department contracts are awarded to large firms, even though new ideas are usually generated by small companies. The contracts tend to go to the same firms over the years, encouraging them merely to improve existing products. Technological progress, however, requires breakthroughs arrived at by rejecting old ideas.

Soviet scientists point to the Japanese example of the strength of civilian research. Despite, or probably because of, the absence of military research and development, Japan managed to reach the U.S. level of technological advancement. Comparisons of Japan and the United States provide convincing evidence that direct civilian studies are more cost-effective than spin-offs from military R&D programs.[23] Military research yields few results that translate directly into civilian uses. Only 20 percent of the results of military research and development have been applied in the civilian sector.[24] Only 7 percent of patents from military research contracts, as opposed to 50 percent of all patents, can be used commercially.[25] Indeed, civilian research produces more by-products used for military purposes than vice versa.[26]

The reason for this lies, in part, in the difficulty of diffusing knowledge when military research is shrouded in secrecy. More pertinent is the fact that military technology is too sophisticated, or simply inappropriate, for civilian uses. There is no need to employ stealth technology in civilian aviation, and possible civilian applications for SDI's exotic technologies are difficult to imagine.

Given SDI's deleterious effect on the U.S. economy, the United States was keen to involve foreign firms in the SDI research program. The participation of allied countries in SDI, according to Soviet experts, provided additional intellectual and technological resources for U.S. military purposes. It also served to prevent Western Europe and Japan from achieving greater technological progress and becoming more competitive.[27]

In addition to stifling technological progress and economic growth, SDI showed little promise of producing an effective and affordable ballistic missile defense. Soviet scientists had determined, as early as 1985, that countermeasures to BMD could be built more quickly and cheaply than the defense system.[28] They concluded that the possibility of creating an ABM system that fulfilled the crucial "Nitze criterion" of being cost-effective at the margin was "extremely doubtful."[29] Even if SDI research were affordable, the cost of development and deployment seemed prohibitive. U.S. budgetary constraints, Rogov asserted, precluded the introduction of new weapon systems, including ballistic missile defenses, unless other defense appropriations were cut. He estimated that deployment of an ABM system in space would require additional funding of $15-20 billion each year, which would necessitate large reductions in other defense programs.[30]

Soviet officials displayed unease at the possible military spin-offs from the exotic technologies undergoing research in the SDI program. They feared that discoveries from SDI would be employed to develop a new generation of weapons and of command and control systems.[31] Concern about the application of SDI to other arms programs induced the USSR initially to try to constrain SDI research.

Moreover, deployment of even small-scale defenses could imperil strategic stability. The introduction of BMD would complicate mutual deterrence and render the strategic balance more precarious. Creation of a BMD system would stimulate the deployment of countermeasures, which in turn would generate strong incentives for further buildup of offensive arms.[32] The introduction of a limited defense would reduce fear of retaliation, thereby encouraging adventuresome American behavior and increasing the risk of nuclear war. Renunciation of the ABM Treaty would cause Soviet-American relations to deteriorate.[33] Therefore, Soviet diplomacy was aimed at preserving strategic stability by preventing the erosion of the ABM Treaty. Soviet negotiators insisted on banning SDI development and deployment in order to keep the ABM Treaty intact.

The prospects for averting an arms race in space improved during the late 1980s because of qualified support in the administration and Congress for SDI. From the beginning, American political figures set different aims for the SDI program. Gorbachev affirmed the conviction that "in Washington there are at least ten cynics for every 'believer' in the surrealistic plan of salvation from the nuclear threat." Officials endorsed SDI for a variety of motives: to create a limited antimissile defense that would reduce American susceptibility to retaliation, to undermine the USSR's economy by drawing it into the space race, to generate huge profits, or to ensure West European dependence on the United States.[34] The consensus behind SDI was considered tenuous. Alexei Arbatov argued that "the coalition supporting the Strategic Defense Initiative is far from monolithic. Given a certain turn of events, it could fall apart or lose its influence."[35] Soviet policy could encourage some U.S. politicians to abandon support for SDI.

The backing of SDI among moderate Republicans, in the Soviet view, was limited. These moderates envisaged the creation of small-scale ABM systems. They wanted SDI research to be confined to laboratories and advocated continued compliance with the ABM Treaty. Moderate Republicans, Soviet observers noted, also favored cuts in strategic weapons. After the Reykjavik summit, they exhibited concern that deployment of BMD would render impossible a reduction in offensive arms.[36] The Soviet position on space weapons was designed to entice pragmatists in the U.S. government to support a grand compromise trading reductions in offensive forces for restrictions on the development of defensive arms.[37]

Soviet experts observed that a majority in Congress favored SDI research that complied with the strict interpretation of the ABM Treaty, but showed little support for testing, development, or deployment of SDI components or systems.[38] In fact, the U.S. Congress generally approved of SDI but did not share Reagan's ambitious goals for the program. Although Congress appropriated less money than the administration requested, it consistently increased funding for SDI, from $1.4 billion in FY1985 to $3.8 billion in FY1990, at a time when overall defense spending was leveling off. Congressional opposition was directed mainly at the scope of the SDI program. Most members of Congress came out against the grandiose plan to render nuclear weapons obsolete and preferred a point defense system that would protect only military forces and thus enhance nuclear deterrence.

The Reagan administration's broad interpretation of the ABM Treaty incurred harsh criticism. In March 1987, Senator Sam Nunn issued a report reaffirming the traditional understanding of the treaty. He threatened a showdown with the administration if it altered the official government position. Reagan averted confrontation with the Congress by agreeing to abide by the narrow interpretation of the ABM Treaty.

The Soviet Union thus saw little chance to stop SDI research outright but found influential allies in the United States willing to preserve the ABM Treaty. In spite of vigorous support for SDI by some political figures, Oleg Bykov suggested, the combination of improved Soviet-American relations and domestic opposition to SDI could remove SDI as an obstacle to nuclear arms reduction and perhaps bring an end to the program.[39]

The chances of settling differences over antiballistic missiles were improved by the changing direction of the SDI research. By 1988, U.S. efforts began to switch from space-based technology to earth-based.[40] The United States was abandoning attempts to build an impenetrable shield in favor of point defense. The aim of the SDI program became the creation of an ABM system of limited effectiveness, mainly ground-based, designed to defend not the population but American strategic forces.[41]

At the end of the Reagan administration, the United States had not yet achieved results from SDI enabling it to decide on full-scale development. This, Soviet officials concluded, left time to prevent the extension of the arms race to outer space.[42] The prospects for reaching agreement on strategic defense were enhanced by the Bush administration, which was losing interest in SDI.[43]

The reassuring trends evident in the second Reagan administration grew more pronounced during the Bush presidency. Bush announced his intention in May 1989 to move beyond a policy of containment, and in October, Secretary of State Baker expressed the administration's interest in seeing *perestroika* succeed. The four-part agenda of superpower dialogue was expanded to a five-part agenda to include global problems. Soviet leaders began discussing their economic programs and difficulties with their American counterparts. The December summit in Malta gave precedence to economic issues and initiated a process of close consultation between the two leaders over the changes in Europe. Soviet observers were heartened by American moderation. They welcomed the Bush administration's commitment to preserving stability during the political transition and its decision to refrain from seeking unilateral advantage from the East European revolutions.[44]

With American backing, the USSR gained observer status in the General Agreement on Tariffs and Trade. The June 1990 Washington summit augmented superpower cooperation with accords on a range of issues, from civil aviation and drug trafficking to drastic reductions in chemical weapon stockpiles and verification procedures for two unratified treaties on nuclear testing. It produced a trade agreement that, in Gorbachev's view, promised modest economic benefits but attested to tangible U.S. support for Soviet reform.[45] Reporting to the Supreme Soviet on his visit to the United States, Gorbachev characterized Soviet-American relations as the beginning of cooperation with elements of partnership.[46]

The Bush administration planned to cut the defense budget, which appeared to confirm Soviet predictions that fiscal constraints would prevent deployment of SDI. President Bush announced that he did not anticipate making a decision on SDI deployment before 1992, and enthusiasm for creating a modern ABM system was waning. Under these conditions, the Gorbachev leadership was prepared to relinquish efforts to obtain a legal commitment to preserve the strict interpretation of the ABM Treaty and was ready to proceed with reductions in strategic offensive arms.

RESTRUCTURING EUROPEAN SECURITY

Soviet policy toward Western Europe changed its emphasis under Gorbachev, in accordance with the precept of new thinking, to safeguarding security through political means. Rather than trying to dominate, with Soviet military might, the threat emanating from the other side of the continent, as had been done in the past, the Gorbachev leadership sought to alleviate it by removing sources of hostility and reducing military potentials. Downgrading the importance of military aspects of relations in Europe made the Soviet Union feel safer and allowed it to expand cooperation with the West.

The elimination of nuclear weapons in Europe was proclaimed as the ultimate aim of Soviet policy.[47] The more immediate objective was to reduce and eventually to remove the U.S. nuclear presence on the continent. Nuclear disarmament in Europe served to weaken NATO's offensive capabilities and to demilitarize relations between the blocs. Western Europe was more interested than was the United States in developing cooperation with the Soviet Union but was constrained by its reliance on U.S. security guarantees. Cuts in nuclear forces were expected to reinforce U.S. tendencies toward decreasing military involvement in Europe and to increase West European influence over security arrangements. Greater West European authority over its own defense, encouraged by Soviet assurances, raised the prospects for gradually reducing West European dependence on American nuclear commitments and creating alternative security structures based on East-West cooperation. Thus, Soviet leaders hoped, by alleviating military tensions, to provide Western Europe with greater scope to strengthen ties with the Soviet Union.

Conventional wisdom in Moscow holds that Western Europe generally shows more interest than does the United States in constructive dialogue with the USSR.[48] At the same time, European participants in NATO's military organization continue to rest their security on U.S. nuclear guarantees,[49] which impedes West European efforts to increase interaction with the East. Improvement in U.S.-Soviet relations facilitates the reduction of tensions in Europe. Bovin asserts that the ability of the USSR to achieve its objectives of lowering the intensity of military confrontation in Europe and promoting economic and scientific cooperation is to a considerable extent contingent upon U.S. policy.[50] During periods of global tension, Western Europe places greater stock in American commitments, offering more support for U.S. security policy and curbing ties with socialist countries. The United States, according to Aleksandr Yakovlev, had in the past promoted confrontation partly to tighten allied discipline and to subordinate West European concerns to its own.[51]

Yuri Davydov of the USA Institute explains how improving superpower relations helps to alleviate tensions in Europe. The influence of Western Europe, he argues, stems from its economic capacity. In military terms, West European countries are dependent on the United States. When confrontation mounts, as in the early 1980s, the importance of military factors grows, which increases West European attachment to the United States. Conversely, when tensions diminish, so does the weight of security considerations, and Western Europe acquires greater scope to assert its own interests. The resumption of the superpower dialogue in 1985, Davydov notes, allowed Western Europe to expand cooperation with the East.[52]

The establishment of constructive interaction between the United States and the Soviet Union obviated the need to pin hopes on Western Europe to help moderate U.S. security policy. Even when West European governments disagreed with U.S. policy, they sometimes lacked sufficient influence to affect American decisions. For instance, West European opposition managed to do little to curb the SDI program. Soviet officials up to the mid-1980s had regularly urged Western Europe to use its position in NATO to restrain U.S. actions.[53] Soviet observers noted that despite some backing for SDI in Western Europe, all major West European governments were critical of the program.[54] They feared that SDI would cause a rift between American and West European security interests, encouraging the United States, in the event of hostilities, to try to confine nuclear war to Europe, and rendering U.S. nuclear pledges less reliable. If the United States were protected by ballistic missile defenses, its foreign policy would become more adventurous and as a result would have a damaging effect on the arms control process and on East-West relations. Furthermore, Britain and France were concerned that a superpower competition in BMD might undermine the credibility of their nuclear deterrents.[55]

However, notwithstanding their opposition to SDI, West European governments were unwilling or unable to exert effective pressure on the Reagan administration to modify the program. As NATO was engrossed in debate over SDI in 1985, Gorbachev made his first Western visit as general secretary to France, then a leading skeptic regarding SDI. The trip produced no tangible results on the issue. In the following months, Britain, West Germany, and Italy signed agreements with the U.S. government to participate in SDI research. Soviet experts saw that West European governments strongly favored the preservation of the ABM Treaty, but were unsure what impact that would have. Some Soviet analysts, without venturing to predict the outcome of disagreements in NATO over SDI, recalled the tendency of the United States to make major decisions on security issues, particularly on antimissile systems, without consulting its allies.[56] In a congenial atmosphere of warm superpower relations, the Soviet Union could deal directly with the United States to resolve the dispute over defensive weapons rather than attempt to put indirect pressure through Western Europe on the United States to compromise.

Improvement in the climate of Soviet-American relations also facilitated a possible weakening of U.S. military commitments to NATO. The Soviet leadership saw little hope of driving the United States out of Western Europe. Gorbachev insisted repeatedly that the USSR accepted U.S. involvement in Western Europe.[57] Some Soviet commentators expect the United States to maintain a nuclear presence in Europe.[58]

Nevertheless, Soviet analysts perceive a growing inclination of the United States to scale back its military engagement in Europe. Atlanticism, to them, appears to be on the decline, as the United States begins to lose interest in Western Europe, especially in shouldering part of the burden of West European defense.[59] According to Sergei Karaganov, deputy director of the Institute of Europe, the new consensus in Washington, including among Atlanticists, directs the United States to pressure its allies to spend more for their defense by threatening to withdraw troops from the continent. Furthermore, the U.S. government seeks to reduce the emphasis on nuclear weapons in NATO strategy in an effort to distance itself from a potential war in Europe.[60]

A decrease in U.S. military involvement in Europe is seen by Soviet experts to contribute to Soviet security. Reliance on U.S. assurances constrains West European actions in the security field, which hinders Soviet attempts to stabilize the military balance. Greater West European input in NATO policy raises the prospects for East-West security cooperation on the continent. The deployment of SS-20s had the effect, which was damaging to Soviet security, of strengthening the strategic link between the United States and Western Europe. In the view of Gorbachev and his associates, Soviet interests were better served by eliminating intermediate-range missiles (IRMs) and thereby weakening transatlantic military ties.

Even after the Intermediate- and Short-Range Missile Treaty was signed in December 1987, many proponents of new thinking claimed that the original deployment of SS-20s had been justified by the need to achieve nuclear parity in Europe. The European nuclear balance became equal only after SS-20 missiles appeared, and the introduction of Pershing-2 and Tomahawk cruise missiles would have proceeded regardless of what the USSR did.[61] From a strictly military standpoint, the SS-20 decision was sound.[62] The mistake of the decision, Soviet experts argued, lay in underestimating its political ramifications.[63] The main point of contention among Soviet officials during the INF negotiations, and among Soviet commentators writing postmortems on the SS-20 ordeal, was the price the USSR should have paid to keep the U.S. missiles out of Europe.[64]

The Gorbachev leadership was prepared to pay a higher price than its predecessors to eliminate intermediate-range missiles because it assigned higher priority to generating East-West cooperation than to seeking a favorable military balance in Europe. Following the logic of new thinking, Soviet reformers believed that the success of *perestroika*, more than the outcome of military confrontation, would determine the future of the Soviet Union. So, Soviet arms levels had to be reduced in order to reallocate resources at home and to diminish impediments to Soviet interaction with the economies and societies of Western Europe. Moreover, new thinking maintained that the outside world is responsive to conciliatory Soviet behavior. Shifts in Western policy demonstrated that the West could be influenced to some degree in overcoming its enmity toward the USSR.[65]

Advocates of new thinking attached overriding importance to eliminating U.S. IRMs in Europe. Gorbachev and his supporters were far more preoccupied with removing obstacles to improved security relations in Europe than with achieving a favorable alignment of nuclear forces. The Brezhnev and Andropov leaderships were obsessed by the imminent arrival of Pershing-2s and GLCMs on the continent, but they accorded higher priority to gaining advantage in the nuclear balance. They rejected the zero option in 1981 and were slow to offer low equal ceilings on IRMs because they were primarily concerned with offsetting the nuclear potentials of all NATO countries with Soviet theater nuclear forces.[66] In contrast, new thinkers sought first and foremost to weaken the strategic link between Western Europe and the United States so that security arrangements in Europe could be made safer for the Soviet Union.

The Brezhnev Politburo's attempts to establish unilaterally what it considered to be nuclear parity in Europe had reinforced Western Europe's inclination to rest its security on U.S. guarantees. When the USSR, in the late 1970s, matched American strategic capabilities, Western Europe began to lose confidence in U.S. security pledges. Strategic parity undermined extended deterrence. Western Europe saw no attractive alternative to existing security arrangements and therefore sought to restore the credibility of American assurances.[67] By the late 1970s, West European governments were already intent on augmenting the strategic link to the United States. Soviet buildup of theater nuclear weapons only confirmed that intention. By depriving NATO of its capacity for escalation dominance, the Soviet introduction of SS-20s encouraged West European leaders to come out in favor of Pershing-2 and cruise missile deployments.[68]

The heads of West European countries, Soviet analysts argued, attached fundamental value to participation in NATO's nuclear planning and to maintaining U.S. nuclear weapons on the continent. Pershing-2 and GLCM deployments strengthened the nuclear ties of the allies to the United States.[69] The major West European members of NATO seemed determined to preserve some form of nuclear deterrent. For this reason, they appeared anxious at the prospect of eliminating IRMs.[70]

As the ISRM negotiations were nearing completion, the Soviet Union encountered resistance from West European governments to nuclear disarmament. These governments, Karaganov remarked, showed greater interest in arms talks themselves than in concrete measures of arms reduction, and once agreement was about to be reached, their "enthusiasm for disarmament change[d] into evasiveness, and then into direct hostility."[71] Davydov attributed the anxiety of West European governments at the proposed removal of IRMs from Europe to their fear of rupturing the strategic link that, they believed, held the alliance together.[72] They were worried about separating their security interests from those of the United States because, in spite of the doubts about the value of U.S. nuclear guarantees, they saw no adequate substitutes to American military commitments.[73]

The conclusion of the ISRM Treaty pulled away the crutch of West European countries and obliged them to reconsider their security arrangements. Soviet leaders hoped to furnish assurances that might compensate in part for NATO's nuclear ties. The combination of disarmament and an improved political climate in Europe offered some possibility that West European reliance on U.S. nuclear pledges might be weakened. Karaganov recalled that détente had allayed the fears of West Europeans, made their lingering doubts about U.S. guarantees relatively less significant, and on the whole reduced the importance of military matters in East-West relations.[74] Warming relations and disarmament could reinforce each other in a process that tempered Western Europe's perceived need to rest its security on American assurances and provided it with more scope to expand its ties to socialist countries.

In fact, the ISRM Treaty produced a burgeoning in Soviet-West European relations. Soviet diplomacy, which had concentrated on the United States, shifted focus in 1988 to Western Europe. Government contacts, from summit meetings to visits of parliamentarians and military officials, grew substantially. The Soviet

Union developed wide-ranging cooperation with West European countries, including bilateral and multilateral agreements on information and cultural exchanges, the environment, food production, and management training, as well as investment treaties and efforts to harmonize legal norms. The Foreign Ministry established a new department for security and cooperation in Europe to expand Soviet involvement. Although the USSR attached great importance to its relations with the United States, it derived larger benefits from its connections to Western Europe.[75]

By modifying the existing basis of NATO security structures, the elimination of IRMs improved the prospects for East-West security cooperation. The ISRM Treaty, Davydov asserted, undermined West European fears of the Soviet Union and trust in the Atlantic Alliance. The Pershing-2 and cruise missiles embodied the extension of deterrence to Europe, and their removal shook confidence in the American guarantee, causing West European leaders to question the value of NATO and of U.S. leadership.[76] Military alliances are maintained by external threats. Once the USSR presented less of a danger, the West was unsure how to respond. The ISRM Treaty fractured the consensus on security among NATO countries. While some members of the West European establishment wanted to shore up nuclear deterrence or to accelerate West European military integration, others were prepared to countenance the creation of a new security order. Disagreements within NATO, Davydov concluded, offered a real possibility for reconstituting the security structure of Europe.[77]

Karaganov affirmed the belief that hardly anyone considered the concept of extended deterrence credible.[78] The "foundations of the old security system have been crumbling," he stated, ever since the Soviet achievement of strategic parity. American nuclear commitments have been "virtually an empty shell" and the alliance has "entered a period of profound structural crisis." The weakening of security relations within NATO, Karaganov contended, provided "unprecedented opportunities" for radically lowering the level of military confrontation in Europe and mitigating the military division of the continent.[79]

As compensation for the diminishing reliability of U.S. nuclear assurances, Western Europe, mainly at the urgings of France, accelerated its process of military integration. This process, according to some Soviet analysts, was designed to create a "European buttress" for NATO,[80] to increase the leverage of West European nations inside the alliance.[81] Greater West European influence might be used to promote disarmament or, alternatively, to persuade the United States to uphold nuclear deterrence.[82] Other experts described the purpose of military integration as decreasing West European dependence for security on the United States.[83] The growing independence of Western Europe was expected to assist in reducing the scale of military preparations in Europe.[84]

In spite of the concern shown by Soviet experts, they did not foresee West European military integration as compensating adequately for U.S. security commitments. In particular, they saw only a remote possibility that France would extend nuclear guarantees to West Germany. Some viewed this possibility with apprehension,[85] but others discounted it, asserting that France had no intention of replacing U.S. nuclear guarantees.[86]

The diminished credibility of American security commitments and the inability of Western Europe to find a suitable substitute for them was expected to encourage pan-European security cooperation. With a view to creating a new security system, the USSR began to offer concrete proposals for a common European home. Soviet foreign affairs specialists envisioned a lengthy process of erecting the common European house by transcending the existing bloc structures. They argued that the transatlantic ties in NATO provided stability,[87] particularly in the face of the uncertainties following the revolutions in Eastern Europe.[88] While the United States sustained a military presence, Zhurkin explained, growing East-West cooperation would dilute the military content of the alliances and knock down barriers that divide the continent. Military structures would wither away as the blocs transformed themselves into strictly political alliances. European-wide contacts and consultations would turn increasingly into permanent ties and eventually solidify into institutions, perhaps into supranational organizations for the whole of Europe.[89] The transition to a new security order would take at least ten years.[90]

The Soviet Union is developing the social and economic components of the common European home by accepting Western standards of interaction and forging strong links to Western institutions. Soviet diplomats express interest in acceding to the conventions of the Council of Europe, an organization based on pluralist democracy.[91] The USSR had insisted that the European Community (EC) treat the Council for Mutual Economic Assistance (CMEA) as a bloc. With official recognition of the EC in August 1988, the Soviet government gave consent to the conclusion of bilateral accords between the EC and CMEA members and paved the way for the broad set of Soviet agreements with the EC signed in December 1989. Soviet economic integration into Europe, Soviet analysts maintain, can begin once domestic reform is carried out.[92]

The Gorbachev leadership plans to build a pan-European security system by strengthening and enlarging the scope of the Conference on Security and Cooperation in Europe. Gorbachev finds great similarities between Soviet and Western notions of the European home but dislikes the Bush administration's concept of "Europe whole and free," which would place NATO at the center of the European order rather than erect a completely new structure.[93] He prefers to expand the authority of CSCE so as to balance the security interests of East and West while maintaining the involvement of the United States and Canada in Europe. The USSR therefore wants CSCE to institute regular summit and foreign ministers meetings, to establish a secretariat and to continue to sponsor negotiations on disarmament and confidence building measures.

Soviet officials designed a new security system both to promote extensive cooperation and to preserve Soviet influence on the continent. Arms reductions that enhanced stability served to alleviate Western concerns, to weaken public support within the alliance countries for NATO's nuclear policy and to create conditions facilitating change in existing security arrangements. The huge armed forces of the Soviet Union, Gorbachev acknowledged to the Council of Europe in July 1989, had obstructed Soviet participation in European developments.[94] Yuri Davydov added that Soviet defense cuts, especially reductions in nuclear weapons, would assuage NATO's worries about the USSR's domination of European security structures.[95]

By 1990, Gorbachev and his advisors were preoccupied far less with removing obstacles to Soviet-West European interaction than with decreasing the Soviet sense of insecurity aroused by the rapidly changing political landscape. The revolutions in Eastern Europe stimulated the construction of the common European house[96] and improved the prospects for a collective European security system,[97] but raised the risks of instability[98] and eroded Soviet influence. Analysts such as Davydov were adamant that the military balance should be maintained and were noticeably uneasy about the declining Soviet capacity to shape events on the continent.[99]

German unification proceeded at a fast pace following the March 1990 elections in the German Democratic Republic. The Soviet leadership, determined to minimize the damaging impact on Soviet security of the political upheavals in Europe, opposed the military strengthening of NATO through the incorporation of East Germany. Gorbachev insisted that the merger of the two Germanies should not upset the European balance and should be "synchronized" with the creation of the common European home through arms reductions and adjustments in the alliance systems.[100] The Soviet position, Shevardnadze specified, was contingent upon changes in NATO strategy, disarmament, and the development of pan-European security structures.[101] He expected German unification to be accompanied by nuclear force cuts and an undertaking by the new state to renounce any aspirations of acquiring nuclear weapons.[102] Chancellor Kohl proved forthcoming. His concessions on these matters, as well as the revisions in military doctrine announced at the July 1990 NATO summit meeting, were instrumental in surmounting Soviet reservations about the inclusion of a united Germany in NATO. He forswore the manufacture, possession and control of nuclear weapons, promised to decrease the number of German troops and pledged not to deploy nuclear arms in the former territory of East Germany.[103]

The Soviet Union is less interested in reducing British and French nuclear forces than in lowering the level of American nuclear weapons in Europe. The USSR persists in its efforts, despite staunch resistance, to bring Britain and France into the disarmament process. Attempts to include third party nuclear forces in the INF talks blocked agreement. Soviet offers to negotiate directly with the European nuclear powers were rebuffed. Britain and France, the Soviet government hoped, would alter their stance once a Strategic Arms Reduction Treaty had been concluded,[104] and they informed Gorbachev that they would enter negotiations after Soviet and American strategic stockpiles had been cut by 50 percent.[105] Soviet experts proceed on the assumption that Britain and France would cut their arsenals proportionately to the superpowers. The resulting superiority in numbers of weapons possessed by NATO members would be acceptable to the USSR.[106] The Soviet government favors negotiations among all of the countries that deploy tactical nuclear weapons, but its immediate aim lies in reducing American systems. Since Britain and France are unwilling to participate, Soviet officials express a readiness to begin with bilateral U.S.-Soviet TNW talks that would include third party nuclear forces at a later stage.[107]

The Gorbachev leadership has repeatedly given way to British and French refusals to join arms control negotiations because the success of its policy towards Europe is contingent to a much greater extent on the reduction of the U.S. nuclear presence. Soviet analysts note that the West European nuclear powers regard their arsenals as important means for enhancing their international prestige.[108] The British deterrent reinforces NATO's doctrine of flexible response but could be used independently in a way that complicates American strategy.[109] French nuclear forces serve not only to deter the USSR but also to gain autonomy from the United States, to offset superior German economic strength and to exert influence in Europe.[110] The creation of a new security system on the continent is impeded far less by third-party nuclear arms than by West European reliance on U.S. nuclear guarantees. In particular, dependence on the transatlantic nuclear link tempers German interest in security cooperation with the Soviet Union. Therefore, the USSR has pressed for cuts in TNWs to alter security arrangements in Europe by releasing Germany and the rest of Western Europe from the constraints imposed by American commitments.

Germany is the member of NATO most disposed towards reductions in TNWs.[111] German officials are worried that in a conflict, nuclear arms might explode only on German soil,[112] so there is broad support in all political parties for the elimination of battlefield nuclear systems.[113] By Soviet interpretation, Germany's inability to acquire nuclear weapons places it at a disadvantage. It wants to decrease the military component of relations on the continent so that it can flex its economic muscle. However, it seeks to maintain Western backing while forging stronger ties to the East and hesitates to rid itself of nuclear arms in the absence of an attractive alternative to American assurances.[114]

The Soviet proposal for a double zero had caused rifts in the governing center-right coalition of the Federal Republic of Germany. The government later was divided over the issue of tactical nuclear forces. Chancellor Kohl favored their modernization. The Free Democrats and some Christian Democrats were opposed. Foreign Minister Genscher's faction won out and in March 1988, the FRG persuaded NATO to postpone a decision on replacing the Lance missile. The following year, Kohl again refused to back Lance modernization, and extracted a commitment from the alliance to commence negotiations on TNWs once an agreement reducing conventional weapons was reached.

President Bush, according to Soviet experts, wanted a successor for Lance so as to nip the prospect of a third zero in the bud and thereby to retain West European dependence on U.S. security guarantees and to prevent the emergence of a new security system in Europe.[115] Britain approved of the American position, and France stood midway between West Germany and the United States. Although France was adamant on preserving its nuclear deterrent, it appreciated the need for disarmament to restore unity on the continent.[116]

The Gorbachev leadership was counting on West Germany to provide momentum in the Atlantic alliance to cut tactical nuclear weapons. Playing on fears of nuclear exchanges confined to Germany, the USSR proposed the withdrawal of TNWs from the inter-German border[117] and invited the FRG into TNW talks.[118] Soviet analysts suggest that reductions could begin with the elimination of TNWs in central Europe.[119] The Soviet Union is trying to entice Germany to press for the quick removal of battlefield nuclear systems and to block NATO's modernization program at a time when opposition is mounting in Germany to the deployment of tactical air-to-surface missiles (TASM).

Gorbachev and his advisors expected conventional arms cuts to draw the West into TNW reductions. The Atlantic alliance regards TNWs as a means to offset the Warsaw Pact's preponderance of conventional forces, so the achievement of parity would call into question the West's justification for relying on nuclear arms.[120] Since NATO used TNW to deter a conventional as well as nuclear attack,[121] decreasing Soviet offensive capabilities was particularly important in persuading the United States to engage in TNW negotiations.

The Warsaw Pact in July 1988 called for a new set of conventional arms talks aimed at diminishing offensive potentials.[122] Gorbachev demonstrated his readiness to make asymmetrical cuts by announcing in December the unilateral withdrawal of a half million men and of six out of thirty Soviet tank divisions from Eastern Europe. At the opening of the CFE talks in March 1989, the Soviet delegation put forward an initiative to eliminate advantages on both sides and to weaken offensive capabilities before proceeding to lower substantially the level of armaments. The

CFE Treaty will decrease greatly the Soviet capacity for attack by imposing disproportionately large reductions on the Warsaw Pact, preventing massive concentrations of ground forces, and limiting Soviet personnel and equipment stationed outside Soviet territory and inside the western USSR.

The Soviet government was prepared from June 1986 to discuss TNWs within the context of conventional disarmament. In January 1988, Shevardnadze proposed the inclusion of dual-capable weapons in the conventional arms talks and the limitation of nuclear charges through separate negotiations.[123] He was eager to begin TNW talks right away. The start of the CFE process raised Soviet expectations that the United States would agree to address the TNW issue. The Warsaw Pact Foreign Ministers asserted that reductions in conventional forces and tactical nuclear weapons would reinforce each other,[124] but the West was unwilling to make cuts in TNWs until the Soviet Union relinquished conventional superiority. NATO's May 1989 commitment to initiate TNW negotiations once a conventional arms accord was reached showed Soviet officials that the rapid conclusion of CFE offered the fastest means to get TNW reductions underway.

Gorbachev and his associates discerned positive developments in the West. They applauded NATO's shift of emphasis from the military to the political content of the alliance.[125] They acclaimed the growing contacts between NATO and the Warsaw Pact as well as the steps taken by the United States to avoid making the transformation of Europe threatening to Moscow. After the NATO summit of July 1990 enunciated revisions in strategy, declaring that nuclear arms would only be employed as a last resort, Shevardnadze stated that the West was beginning to retract its doctrine of flexible response.[126]

Soviet analysts were heartened by modifications in the Atlantic alliance's nuclear modernization program and deterrent posture. NATO was shifting priority from battlefield to longer-range weapons.[127] Bush's cancellation in May 1990 of plans for a Lance follow-on and of the development of new nuclear artillery left only the upgrading of air-based systems, the development of a tactical air-to-surface missile to replace gravity bombs. The West was abandoning its integrated strategy of using nuclear forces alongside conventional arms and was opting for a "politicized" deterrent posture that assigns TNWs an important role in preventing war but excludes the possibility of conducting combat operations with nuclear weapons. Although NATO plans to introduce TASMs and to keep a nuclear arsenal in Europe even after a conventional balance is established, it is prepared to reduce TNWs to a minimum. The resulting implementation of a no-early-first-use policy, in the judgment of Soviet experts, would engender greater stability.[128]

Minimum deterrence in Europe serves Soviet interests. Soviet foreign affairs specialists observe that NATO considers nuclear weapons essential to avert war and to preserve alliance unity, so it firmly rejects the idea of a third zero. Since the fear of a U.S. withdrawal is one of the chief stimulants to West European military integration, the complete removal of U.S. nuclear guarantees could ultimately damage Soviet interests. The presence of a small number of nuclear weapons provides stability. Therefore, Soviet analysts argue, the elimination of TNWs should wait until the European security system is rebuilt and the instabilities in Eastern Europe and the USSR are overcome.[129] Retaining some TNWs can ease the transition to a new European security order.

Nuclear arms control furthered the Gorbachev leadership's aims of lowering military competition, engendering greater stability, and fostering cooperative relations with the West. These aims dictated the need for substantial Soviet concessions to promote arms reduction but also set the limits for progress in negotiations. In general, nuclear weapons cuts assuaged Western security concerns and thereby removed impediments to East-West interaction. Large reductions in strategic arsenals augmented the constructive dialogue with the United States. Tacit U.S. restraints on SDI development prevented a race in space weapons, which could rupture superpower relations. Elimination of intermediate- and short-range nuclear missiles in Europe diminished Western

Europe's reliance on U.S. security commitments and raised the prospects for overcoming entirely the division of the continent.

Soviet recognition of Western interest in retaining nuclear weapons tempered Soviet insistence on disarmament in some areas. Continued U.S. support for SDI research indicated the benefits of compromise. Soviet obstinacy on defensive arms could have rekindled Western enmity at a time when the U.S. government was losing its enthusiasm for ABM systems. Similarly, Soviet demands to remove all U.S. tactical nuclear forces from Europe would at best come to nought and at worst raise Western suspicions. Appreciation for the belief of NATO leaders in the stabilizing role of U.S. nuclear engagement persuaded the USSR to modify its position and to make do with a reduction in stages of TNWs.

NOTES

1. Georgi M. Sturua, "Sovetsko-Amerikanskiye Otnoshenia na Novom Etape" ["Soviet-American Relations in a New Stage"], *Mirovaya Ekonomika i Mezhdunarodnye Otnoshenia (MEMO)*, September 1988, p. 26.

2. Aleksandr Ye. Bovin, "Novoye Myshleniye—Trebovaniye Yadernovo Veka," ["New Thinking—The Demand of the Nuclear Age"], *Kommunist*, no. 10 (July), 1986, p. 123.

3. Maj. Gen. Chaldymov in *Krasnaya Zvezda*, 26 May 1988.

4. *Izvestia*, 7 May 1988.

5. Ibid.

6. Oleg N. Bykov, "Realnaya Vozmozhnost Obuzdania Gonki Vooruzhenny" ["A Real Possibility of Curbing the Arms Race"], *MEMO*, January 1986, p. 14.

7. Oleg N. Bykov, "Novaya Kontseptsia Yadernovo Razoruzhenia" ["A New Concept of Nuclear Disarmament"], *MEMO*, February 1987, p. 11.

8. Georgi A. Arbatov, "Perspektivy Sovetsko-Amerikanskykh Otnosheny" ["Prospects for Soviet-American Relations"], *SShA: Ekonomika, Politika, Ideologia*, June 1985, p. 41.

9. *Pravda*, 17 October 1988.

10. Sturua, "Sovetsko-Amerikanskiye Otnoshenia," pp. 27-28.

11. Ibid.

12. *Pravda*, 26 November 1985.

13. Mikhail S. Gorbachev, *Perestroika* (London: Collins, 1987), p. 218.
14. Vladimir F. Petrovsky, "Strategicheskaya Ravnovesiye—Neobkhodimoye Usloviye Bezopasnovo Mira," ["Strategic Equilibrium—A Necessary Condition for a Secure World"], *SShA*, July 1985, p. 41.
15. Andrei A. Kokoshin, "Diskussy po Tsentralnym Voprosam Voyennoy Politiki SShA," ["Discussions on the Central Questions of the USA's Military Policy"], *SShA*, February 1985, pp. 5–8.
16. For example V. M. Berezhkov "Dve Kontseptsy Bezopasnosti" ["Two Concepts of Security"], *SShA*, April 1987, p. 12, and Dmitri T. Yazov, "The Military Balance of Strength and Nuclear Missile Parity," *International Affairs*, April 1988, p. 17.
17. V. A. Savelyev, "Podzhody v SShA k Dialogu s SSSR" ["Approaches in the USA towards Dialogue with the USSR"], *SShA*, November 1986, pp. 6–8.
18. *Pravda*, 9 September 1986.
19. Oleg N. Bykov, "Novoye Politicheskoye Myshleniye v Deystvy" ["New Political Thinking in Action"], *MEMO*, February 1988, p. 13.
20. Sergei M. Rogov, "Perekhodny Period na Politicheskoy Arene SShA" ["Transition Period in the USA's Political Arena"], *SShA*, March 1988, p. 3.
21. Ibid., pp. 5–6.
22. Lev P. Feoktistov, "Gonka Vooruzheny, Voyna i Nauchno-Tekhnichesky Progress Nesovmestimy" ["The Arms Race, War and Scientific-Technological Progress are Incompatible"], *Kommunist*, no. 15 (October), 1986, pp. 103–04; A. A. Vasilyev and A. A. Konovalov, "Nekotoriye Aspekty Vozdeystvia Programmy SOI na Ekonomiku SShA" ["Some Aspects of the SDI Program's Influence on the USA's Economy"], *SShA*, December 1986, pp. 14–18; and Yevgeni Velikhov, Roald Sagdeyev, and Andrei Kokoshin (eds.), *Weaponry in Space: The Dilemma of Security* (Moscow: Mir, 1986), pp. 140–42.
23. Velikhov, Sagdeyev and Kokoshin, *Weaponry in Space*, p. 142.
24. Feoktistov, "Gonka Vooruzheny," p. 104.
25. Vasilyev and Konovalov, "Nekotoriye Aspekty Vozdeystvia Programmy SOI," p. 16.
26. Ibid., p. 17.
27. Ibid., pp. 19–20.
28. Yevgeni Velikhov and Andrei Kokoshin, "Yadernoye Oruzhiye i Dilemmy Mezhdunarodnoy Bezopasnosti" ["Nuclear Weaponry and Dilemmas of International Security"], *MEMO*, April 1985, p. 39.
29. R. Sagdeyev and S. Rodionov, "K Voprosu o Strategicheskykh i Ekonomicheskykh Posledstviakh SOI" ["To the Question of the Strategic and Economic Consequences of SDI"], *MEMO*, May 1986, p. 16.
30. Rogov, p. 6.

31. Makhmut A. Gareyev, *Sovetskaya Voyennaya Nauka* [Soviet Military Science] (Moscow: Znaniye, 1988), p. 8.
32. Velikhov, Sagdeyev and Kokoshin, *Weaponry in Space*, p. 106.
33. Aleksandr A. Pikayev and Aleksandr G. Savelyev, "Strategicheskaya Oboronnaya Initsiativa: Argumenty Storonnikov: Vozrazhenia Protivnikov" ["Strategic Defense Initiative: Arguments of Supporters and Objections of Opponents"], *MEMO*, December 1988, pp. 67–69.
34. *Pravda*, 8 February 1986.
35. *Izvestia*, 16 November 1985.
36. S. Porshakov, "Respublikanskaya Partia SShA v Seredine 80-kh Godov" ["The U.S. Republican Party in the Middle of the 1980s"], *MEMO*, October 1987, pp. 98–99.
37. In mid-1986, a Soviet analyst disclosed that some Soviet officials preferred to postpone arms control until Reagan left office, while others wanted to test American interest in an offense-defense trade-off. Strobe Talbott, *The Master of the Game* (New York: Knopf, 1988), p. 296.
38. Sergei M. Samuylov, "SOI: Spory Prodolzhayutsya" ["SOI: The Debates Continue"], *SShA*, July 1988, p. 66.
39. Bykov, "Novoye Politicheskoye Myshlenie v Deystvy," pp. 17–18.
40. Roald Sagdeyev, "Science Is a Party to Political Decisions," *International Affairs*, November 1988, p. 28.
41. Pikayev and Savelyev, "Strategicheskaya Oboronnaya Initsiativa," p. 67.
42. Vitali Shabanov, "The Doctrine of Security and Peace," *International Affairs*, November 1988, p. 25.
43. Alexei Arbatov, "Polezneye Razgovor po Sushchestvu" ["A More Useful Conversation in Fact"], *Kommunist Vooruzhennykh Sil*, no. 22 (November), 1989, p. 21.
44. Yuri P. Davydov and Mikhail M. Kozhokin, "Politika SShA v Vostochnoy Evrope" ["The USA's Policy in Eastern Europe"], *SShA*, February 1990, pp. 40–41.
45. *Pravda*, 13 June 1990.
46. Ibid.
47. Gorbachev in *Pravda*, 22 April 1986.
48. For instance, S. A. Ulin, "Krizisnye Yavlenia v NATO" ["Crisis Phenomena in NATO"], *SShA*, April 1986, p. 17.
49. Gennadi V. Kolosov, "Voyenno-Politicheskiye Aspekty Zapadnoevropeyskovo Integratsionnovo Protsessa" ["Military-Political Aspects of the West European Integration Process"], *MEMO*, April 1987, p. 36.
50. *Izvestia*, 20 July 1986.

51. Aleksandr Yakovlev, "Mezhimperialisticheskiye Protivorechia—Sovremenny Kontekst" ["Interimperialist Contradictions—the Contemporary Context"], *Kommunist*, no. 17 (November), 1986, p. 6.
52. Yuri P. Davydov, "Zapadnaya Evropa Posle Zhenevy" ["Western Europe After Geneva"], *SShA*, February 1986, pp. 90–91.
53. Gorbachev in *Pravda*, 8 July 1986.
54. Gennadi A. Vorontsov, "Zapadnaya Evropa i SOI" ["Western Europe and SDI"], *MEMO*, March 1987, p. 43.
55. Sergei A. Karaganov, " 'Zvezdnye Voyny' i Zapadnaya Evropa" [" 'Star Wars' and Western Europe"], *SShA*, May 1986, pp. 32–35.
56. V. A. Mazing and S. K. Oznobishchev, " 'Evropeyskaya Oboronnaya Initsiativa'—Pridatok SOI" [" 'The European Defense Initiative'—An Appendage of SDI"], *SShA*, August 1987, p. 24.
57. Gorbachev declared at the 27th Party Congress (*Pravda*, 26 February 1986) that U.S.–West European ties could not be severed, and included in a joint statement with FRG Chancellor Kohl that the common European home is open to the United States, in *Pravda*, 14 June 1989.
58. Ivan Tyulin and Andrei Zagorsky, "Dimensions of a 'Near-Zero' Nuclear Balance," *International Affairs*, July 1988, p. 114.
59. Anatoli I. Utkin, "Sudby 'Atlantizma' " ["The Fate of 'Atlanticism' "], *SShA*, September 1988, p. 41.
60. Sergei Karaganov, "The USA and the Common European Home," *International Affairs*, August 1989, pp. 17, 19.
61. Georgi M. Sturua, "Bylo li Neobkhodimo Razvertivaniye Raket SS-20?" ["Was the Deployment of SS-20 Missiles Necessary?"], *SShA*, December 1988, pp. 26–27, and Aleksandr Ye. Bovin, "Inye Varianty" ["Other Variants"], *SShA*, December 1988, p. 31.
62. Lev S. Semeyko, "SS-20: Oshibka, no Menshaya, chem Mozhno Bylo by Dumat" ["SS-20: A Mistake, but Smaller than Would Be Thought"], *SShA*, December 1988, p. 34, and Sergei A. Karaganov, "Eshcho Neskolko Soobrazheny" ["Some More Considerations"], *SShA*, December 1988, p. 38.
63. Semeyko, "SS-20," p. 34.
64. Bovin, "Inye Varianty," p. 31; Semeyko, "SS-20," p. 35; and Karaganov, "Eshcho Neskolko Soobrazheny," p. 39.
65. Karaganov, "The USA and the Common European Home," pp. 22, 25.
66. Semeyko, "SS-20," p. 35.
67. Sergei A. Karaganov, "Zapadnaya Evropa, SShA i Problemy Razoruzhenia" ["Western Europe, the USA and Problems of Disarmament"], *SShA*, October 1987, p. 28.
68. Ibid., pp. 29–30.
69. Kolosov, "Voyenno-Politicheskiye Aspekty, p.36."

70. Aleksandr Likhotal, "Na Evropeyskom Napravleny" ["In a European Direction"], *MEMO*, July 1987, pp. 8, 12.

71. Karaganov, "Zapadnaya Evropa, SShA i Problema Razoruzhenia," p. 27.

72. Yuri P. Davydov, "SShA-Zapadnaya Evropa: Bremya Partnerstva" ["USA-Western Europe: The Burden of Partnership"], *SShA*, May 1987, p. 9.

73. Ibid., p. 7.

74. Sergei A. Karaganov, "The Common European Home: The Military Angle," *International Affairs*, August 1988, p. 71.

75. One indication is the Soviet trade turnover of 2.1 billion rubles with the United States compared with 13.7 billion rubles with Britain, France, Italy and West Germany combined. *Narodnoye Khozyaystvo SSSR 1988*, [*The USSR's National Economy 1988*] (Moscow: Finansy i Statistika, 1989) p. 645.

76. Yuri P. Davydov, "SShA, Zapadnaya Evropa i Dogovor po RSD-RMD" ["USA, Western Europe and the ISRM Treaty"], *SShA*, July 1988, pp. 8-9.

77. Ibid., pp. 11-16.

78. Karaganov, "The USA and the Common European Home," p. 24.

79. Karaganov, "The Common European Home: The Military Angle," pp. 76-77.

80. Nikolai Afanasyevsky, Eduard Tarasinkevich, and Andrei Shvedov, "Between Yesterday and Today," *International Affairs*, May 1988, p. 27.

81. Vladimir Stupishin, "Common European Home and the Slogan for a United States of Europe," *International Affairs*, March 1989, p. 93.

82. Ibid.

83. Viktor S. Mikheyev, "SOI i Frantsia" ["SOI and France"], *SShA*, November 1988, p. 24.

84. Anatoli V. Rassadin, "Zapadnoevropeyskaya Voyennaya Integratsia—Perspektivy i Vozmozhnye Posledstvia" ["West European Military Integration—Prospects and Possible Consequences"], *MEMO*, February 1989, pp. 114-15.

85. Afanasyevsky, Tarasinkevich, and Shvedov, "Between Yesterday and Today," p. 27, and Viktor S. Mikheyev, "SShA-Frantsia: Sotrudnichestvo i Protivorechia" ["USA-France: Cooperation and Contradictions"], *SShA*, January 1986, pp. 31-32.

86. Tyulin and Zagorsky, " 'Near-Zero' Nuclear Balance," p. 112.

87. Karaganov, "The USA and the Common European Home," p. 25 and Zhurkin in *Pravda*, 17 May 1989.

88. Pavel Bayev, Vitali Zhurkin, Sergei Karaganov, Viktor Shein, *Tactical Nuclear Weapons in Europe* (Moscow: Novosti, 1990), p. 12.

89. *Pravda*, 17 May 1989.

90. Bayev et al., *Tactical Nuclear Weapons in Europe*, p. 13.
91. Ambassador Yu. B. Kashlev in *Izvestia*, 30 March 1990.
92. Vladimir G. Baranovsky and Vladimir N. Zuyev, "Put k 'Obshcheyevropeyskomu Domu': Ekonomicheskiye Aspekty" ["The Path to a 'Common European Home': Economic Aspects"], *Kommunist*, no. 8 (May), 1989, pp. 109, 117–18.
93. Interview in *Time*, 4 June 1990, p. 33.
94. *Pravda*, 7 July 1989.
95. Yuri P. Davydov, "K Novomu Evropeyskomu Poryadku," To a New European Order, *SShA*, March 1990, pp. 45–46.
96. Gorbachev in *Pravda*, 3 July 1990.
97. Yazov in *Izvestia*, 14 May 1990.
98. Gorbachev in *Pravda*, 5 December 1989.
99. Davydov, "K Novomu Evropeyskomu Poryadku," pp. 44–46.
100. *Pravda*, 21 February 1990.
101. *Izvestia*, 30 May 1990.
102. *Izvestia*, 7 May 1990.
103. *Pravda*, 18 July 1990.
104. Yuli Vorontsov, "The Military-Political Aspects of Security," *International Affairs*, October 1988, p. 41.
105. *Pravda*, 13 June 1990.
106. Tyulin and Zagorsky, " 'Near Zero' Nuclear Balance," p. 113.
107. Sergei V. Kortunov, "Vozmozhny li Peregovory po Takticheskomu Yadernomu Oruzhiyu?" ["Are Negotiations on Tactical Nuclear Weapons Possible?"], *MEMO*, February 1990, pp. 36, 39–40.
108. Aleksandr Pikhayev, "United Kingdom" in Yevgeni M. Primakov (ed.), *IMEMO Disarmament and Security Yearbook 1987* (Moscow: Novosti, 1988), p. 173.
109. Gennadi V. Kolosov, "Velikobritania i Evropeyskaya Bezopasnost: Kontseptsia Natsionalnoy Bezopasnosti i Voyenno-Politichesky Kurs v 80-e Gody," ["Great Britain and European Security: The Concept of National Security and the Military-Political Course in the 1980s"], *MEMO*, May 1990, p. 91.
110. Viktor S. Mikheyev, "Vashington, Parizh i Evropeyskaya Bezopasnost," ["Washington, Paris and European Security"], *SShA*, September 1989, p. 20.
111. Yu. Yudanov, "FRG vo Vtoroy Polovine 80-kh Godov—Osnovnye Problemy i Poiski ikh Reshenia" ["The FRG in the Second Half of the 1980s—Fundamental Problems and the Search for their Solution"], *MEMO*, September 1988, p. 92.
112. Yu. Fe. Fedorov, "OVD i NATO Posle Podpisania Dogovora po RSMD," ["WTO and NATO After the Signing of the ISRM Treaty"], in Yevgeni M. Primakov (ed.), Institut Mirovoy Ekonomiki i Mezhdunarodnykh

Otnoshenia, *Razoruzheniye i Bezopasnost: Ezhegodnik 1988–1989* [IMEMO Disarmament and Security Yearbook 1988–1989] (Moscow: Novosti, 1989), p. 159.

113. Bayev et al., *Tactical Nuclear Weapons in Europe*, p. 18.

114. Yuri P. Davydov, "Nostalgia po 'Sovetskoy Ugroze' " ["Nostalgia for the 'Soviet Threat' "], *SShA*, August 1989, pp. 35–36.

115. Nikolai N. Spasov, "SShA-Zapadnaya Evropa: Novye Bremena," USA-Western Europe: New Burdens, *MEMO*, October 1989, p. 118.

116. Mikheyev, "Vashington, Parizh i Evropeyskaya Bezopasnost," pp. 19–20.

117. *Pravda*, 7 March 1989.

118. *Pravda*, 13 April 1989.

119. Bayev et al., *Tactical Nuclear Weapons in Europe*, p. 45.

120. Ibid., pp. 17–18.

121. Aleksandr G. Savelyev, "Predotvrashcheniye Voyny i Sderzhivaniye: Podkhody OVD i NATO" ["War Prevention and Deterrence: The Approaches of WTO and NATO"], *MEMO*, June 1989, p. 27.

122. *Pravda*, 17 July 1988.

123. *Pravda*, 19 January 1988.

124. *Pravda*, 13 April 1989.

125. *Pravda*, 20 December 1989.

126. *Pravda*, 11 July 1990.

127. Bayev et al., *Tactical Nuclear Weapons in Europe*, pp. 22–23.

128. Ibid., pp. 30–32.

129. Ibid., pp. 14–16.

6

SOVIET CONDUCT OF NUCLEAR ARMS TALKS

New thinking, which mandated reduced Soviet reliance on military power and increased cooperation with the West, impelled the Soviet Union to compromise substantially with the United States to forge progress in nuclear disarmament. The Gorbachev leadership offered the bulk of the concessions required to reach agreement on arms reduction but proved more reluctant to compromise on some issues than others, depending on military and foreign policy objectives. Changes in nuclear strategy and international aims shaped specific Soviet positions on disarmament, determining the way in which the USSR strove to enhance stability.

Gorbachev and his associates gave up Soviet advantages in the number of missiles in the European theater to scale back the U.S. nuclear presence on the continent, thereby lowering the risk of escalation in a European conflict and creating conditions under which European security structures could be rebuilt. They cut first-strike potentials under the START accord, particularly by reducing land-based missiles and placing ceilings on warheads, to strengthen the survivability of retaliatory forces, and they set limits on weapon programs, such as cruise missiles, which they feared might upset the strategic equilibrium. The threat of a continued race to develop technologically advanced arms was diminished by forestalling competition in ballistic missile defenses.

NUCLEAR DISARMAMENT IN EUROPE

Reduction of nuclear weapons in Europe was accomplished mainly at Soviet initiative. Soviet concessions led to agreement on eliminating intermediate-range missiles. From 1987, the Soviet Union forged ahead of the United States in promoting European disarmament, proposing first to get rid of shorter-range missiles and then to begin cutting tactical systems. The Gorbachev leadership aimed to diminish American nuclear engagement in Europe. A devaluation of U.S. nuclear commitments to its transatlantic partners encouraged greater West European independence in charting security policy and raised the prospects of pan-European security structures gradually replacing the NATO military alliance as the basis for West European security.

Prior to their breakdown in 1983, the negotiations on Intermediate-range Nuclear Forces addressed four issues. Two were open to discussion, the other two were not. The USSR demonstrated flexibility on the questions of missile ceilings and of global limits, but insisted on counting British and French nuclear forces and on preventing deployments of Pershing-2s and Tomahawk GLCMs. The Soviet Union was prepared to restrict the number of its SS-20s. It made a series of concessions, eventually offering in October 1983 to go down to 140 missiles, to keep as many warheads as Britain and France possessed. The Soviet government also compromised on the issue of global limits. At first, it rejected U.S. demands to place ceilings on all intermediate-range weapons and argued instead that an accord should cover only nuclear systems in Europe. This would have left available the option of transferring excess SS-20s to the Far East. Later, the Soviet Union agreed to dismantle missiles that would be eliminated by an INF agreement and to freeze deployments of SS-20s in Asia, thus tacitly accepting global limits.

The Soviet Union in the early 1980s was adamant in its determination that British and French weapons should be counted. It had for many years tried to secure compensation for third-party nuclear forces. Soviet negotiators felt that the United

States had ignored this demand long enough and that a prompt settlement was necessary because the European nuclear powers were scheduled to begin upgrading their weapons in the late 1980s. More importantly, the USSR stood firm on the issue of third-party forces in order to prevent the U.S. deployments at an acceptable cost. If British and French nuclear systems were excluded from the talks, the Soviet Union would be obliged to relinquish its virtual monopoly of intermediate-range land-based missiles in Europe. Acceptance of equal ceilings on Soviet and U.S. missiles meant either scrapping all SS-20s or allowing a certain number of Tomahawks. An equal ceiling above zero would require the USSR both to cut back the size of its intermediate-range forces and to permit the American buildup of nuclear arms in Europe.

The fundamental purpose of Soviet participation in the INF talks was to prevent the deployment of Pershing-2s and Tomahawks. This proviso was attached to every single offer made by the USSR. The Soviet position was consistent on this point throughout the course of the negotiations. Just after the Soviet walkout, Georgi Arbatov stated bluntly that "the very essence of the talks has been an effort to avoid the deployment of the American missiles."[1]

Negotiations were resumed in early 1985 under the umbrella Nuclear and Space Talks (NST), whose three components were to be worked out in their interrelationship. Agreement on limiting nuclear forces in Europe was contingent on strategic arms reduction and, more pertinently, on the control of space weapons. Gorbachev's first significant concession was to sever this link and thereby open up the possibility for a separate accord on INF. Gorbachev signalled a willingness to proceed with nuclear disarmament in Europe before settling the other two NST issues, because the INF question was the least complex, providing the greatest chance of successful resolution, and the most urgent. The introduction of Pershing-2 and Tomahawk missiles began in November 1983, whereas the American introduction of new strategic nuclear weapons only got under way in 1985. Also, since increased trade and technological cooperation was expected to come mainly from Western Europe, improving relations with those countries was more pressing than reducing tensions with the United States. Gorbachev relinked ISRM to space weapons from October 1986 to February 1987. This ploy, intended to wrench U.S. concessions on the Strategic Defense Initiative, failed and was quickly abandoned. Gorbachev then returned to seeking a solution to the European missile issue separate from the other two components of NST.

In January 1986, the Soviet Union removed one of the main obstacles to agreement by consenting to exclude British and French nuclear forces from the ISRM negotiations. This concession represented acceptance of equal ceilings on Soviet and American missiles. The USSR would either eliminate all of its SS-20s or sanction the deployment of some Tomahawk GLCMs. In either case, it would relinquish more warheads than the United States. Thus, the USSR offered to make asymmetrical reductions in its European nuclear weapons.

The concession on British and French forces was justified by Shevardnadze at the ratification hearings for the ISRM Treaty with the argument that sticking to the demand to count these forces would have prevented agreement and thereby allowed the United States to retain IRMs in Europe. He claimed that the number of British and French weapons was too small to endanger Soviet security, so the weapons could be safely excluded from negotiations until after the U.S. and Soviet nuclear arsenals had been cut.[2] Pursuing the logic of new thinking, the Soviet Union decided that its nuclear potential need not equal the combined nuclear forces of NATO members. In fact, the Western nuclear powers refused to countenance the inclusion of British and French forces in an ISRM accord. Unless the Soviet Union compromised, it was most unlikely to conclude an agreement with the United States.

In military terms, the Soviet concession was quite affordable. Marshal Akhromeyev acknowledged that the USSR possessed weapons other than SS-20s to compensate for the European nuclear systems.[3] The SS-19 ICBM has a variable range and can be aimed at targets in Western Europe. Britain and France are in the process of building up their forces, so by including these forces in negotiations after START, their modernization can still be constrained.

The Soviet concession on third-party forces involved less the issue as such than the question of equal ceilings. The USSR had tried unsuccessfully to gain compensation for third-party systems in SALT II. In 1981, it placed British and French nuclear arms on the INF agenda, rather than in START, primarily to give credence to its claim that nuclear parity existed in Europe and that the scheduled NATO deployments would upset the balance. Removal of British and French systems from the ISRM talks entailed compromise on the question of equal ceilings. The USSR agreed to cut back the number of its missiles to equal that of the United States and thus to eliminate a larger quantity of weapons. Soviet readiness to make asymmetrical reductions in IRMs indicated that the threat posed by Pershing-2s and Tomahawks in Europe exceeded the value of SS-20s.

Once the USSR had accepted the principle of asymmetrical cuts, instead of proposing a low ceiling on IRMs, it advocated their complete elimination from Europe. The most recent offer was a limit of 140 missiles, amounting to 420 warheads. In October 1986, Gorbachev went straight to zero. He suggested that each side retain 100 warheads on IRMs in Asia and that IRMs be banned entirely from Europe. The Soviet Union clearly preferred to rid Europe of IRMs than to keep some. Indeed, it never had been prepared to sanction NATO's deployments of Pershing-2s and GLCMs, and it was ready to pay a high price to get rid of the missiles once they had been introduced. Shevardnadze defended the USSR's asymmetrical cuts by saying that they were necessary in order to reach zero.[4]

The basic Soviet objective throughout the course of negotiations was the removal of all Pershing-2 and cruise missiles from Europe. The elimination of IRMs in Europe offered military benefits to the Soviet Union. Gorbachev noted that the ISRM

Treaty "would deal a tangible blow to the concepts of limited use of nuclear weapons and the so-called 'controllable escalation' of a nuclear conflict."[5] Defense Minister Yazov endorsed the treaty because it undermined American hopes of achieving victory in a limited nuclear war and benefited Soviet security by removing U.S. missiles capable of striking Soviet territory in eight to ten minutes.[6] Akhromeyev added that despite the fact that the zero option required greater cuts on the Soviet side, it was advantageous because the American missiles could hit the Soviet homeland, but Soviet SS-20s were out of range of U.S. soil.[7]

The political rationale for the zero option was compelling. Elimination of IRMs produced political dividends that exceeded the military advantages of retaining intermediate-range forces. It devalued American extended deterrence, thereby reducing West European reliance on U.S. nuclear commitments and raising West European receptiveness to alternative security arrangements. The weakening of transatlantic nuclear ties was expected to result in increased West European influence within the alliance, which was considered favorable to Soviet interests, and to offer promising opportunities for developing new security structures of a common European home in which Soviet assurances replaced American guarantees in protecting West European security.

In April 1987, the USSR suggested that IRMs be eliminated from Asia. The global zero facilitated verification of the agreement and placed a worldwide ban on GLCMs, a category of weapon in which the United States excelled and that preoccupied Soviet military planners. Shevardnadze noted that although the United States had not yet placed ground-based IRMs in Asia, the global ban prevented it from doing so in the future.[8]

Movement toward the second zero began in 1985. The United States demanded that some restraints be placed on SRMs so that the USSR could not circumvent an INF accord by building up these forces. The Soviet Union already enjoyed superiority in this category of weapon. Gorbachev's plan, announced in January 1986, to rid the world of nuclear weapons by the year 2000 envisaged a fairly early elimination of short-range and tactical nuclear missiles. All IRMs would be removed from Europe in phase one, SRMs and TNWs would be eliminated in phase two as 50 percent cuts in strategic arms were being completed, and in phase three, Britain and France would give up nuclear weapons, while the superpowers eliminated the remaining 50 percent of their nuclear arsenals. At its June 1986 conference in Budapest, the Warsaw Pact announced that Soviet SRMs would be removed from East Germany and Czechoslovakia once U.S. IRMs in Europe were eliminated. In addition, the Warsaw Pact appealed to NATO to reduce short-range and tactical nuclear weapons in tandem with conventional arms cuts.[9] Gorbachev went further at the Reykjavik summit, proposing a freeze on missiles with ranges less than 1,000 kilometers and a new set of negotiations to reduce these forces.

The Soviet Union then proceeded quickly toward the second zero. The USSR announced in February 1987 that it would withdraw its missiles from Czechoslovakia and the GDR as soon as a treaty on European nuclear weapons was signed. In April, Shevardnadze offered to eliminate completely short-range nuclear forces within one year of the treaty's signing, and in July 1987, Gorbachev embraced the double zero, proposing to include in the treaty itself a ban on all SRMs. As it did for IRMs, the Soviet Union bypassed reduced ceilings and went straight to zero. Instead of offering to cut short-range forces, the USSR preferred to ban them entirely.

The Soviet decision to eliminate SRMs was designed primarily to stimulate progress toward a denuclearized Europe. Soviet preponderance in short-range weapons exceeded even that in intermediate-range systems. The USSR relinquished five and one-half times as many SRMs as the United States did. Furthermore, there was no geostrategic asymmetry. Pershing-1s could barely reach Soviet territory. If the superpowers employed SRMs, a nuclear war would be limited for the USSR, as well as for the United States, because neither homeland would be directly affected. However, the Gorbachev leadership was less interested in maintaining the capacity to confine nuclear war to Europe than in scaling back U.S. nuclear engagement. Toward this end the USSR proposed the double zero. Soviet offers up to 1987 bound together short-range and tactical nuclear arms. The two categories of weapons were separated only in April 1987, when the USSR proposed the complete elimination of SRMs. Sensing that this would speed up nuclear disarmament in Europe, the Soviet Union decided first to ban short-range forces and then to tackle the more complex problem of tactical nuclear weapons.

Immediately after the ISRM Treaty was signed, the USSR began pressing hard for a third zero. Soviet leaders stressed the priority of nuclear disarmament[10] and berated NATO for failing to enter negotiations on TNWs. They urged the complete destruction of tactical nuclear arsenals, not only of missiles but also of nuclear capable artillery and tactical aviation. In April 1989, the Soviet Union altered its stance. It shifted emphasis from rapid elimination to gradual reduction of TNWs, calling for TNW talks with a mandate to cut in stages tactical forces in Europe.

The retreat on the third zero reflected Soviet pragmatism. Since NATO was unwilling to eliminate its remaining nuclear arms, the USSR made an offer more likely to prove acceptable. The most immediate Soviet aim was to prevent the modernization of American TNWs. This Soviet concern was apparent when Shevardnadze, on a rare occasion of resorting to the heavy-handed tactics of his predecessor, threatened to respond to the replacement of Lance missiles with Soviet counterdeployments and interruption of the ISRM Treaty's implementation.[11] Commencing negotiations on TNWs would weaken support for the introduction of new American systems in Europe, especially in Germany. Once discussions were taking place, the Soviet Union could present specific initiatives that would undercut NATO's justification for preserving TNWs.

In the TNW talks, which are set to open by 1991, the USSR appears ready to accommodate the main Western objectives. It is likely to approve NATO's proposal to eliminate nuclear artillery.[12] It wants to retain some nuclear missiles[13] but seems prepared to give up its twelve-fold advantage in the number of missiles. A Foreign Ministry official suggested that TNW reductions could begin with the removal of asymmetries.[14] Soviet willingness to make larger reductions than the United States was demonstrated by Shevardnadze's announcement in June 1990 of the unilateral withdrawal of a significant number of Soviet nuclear arms from Eastern Europe.[15] Even though Soviet launchers are dual-capable, and cuts in tactical missiles would constrain the USSR's conventional military potential, the Soviet Union is interested in quickly reaching a TNW agreement by setting a limit on delivery vehicles in the first phase and, only in the second phase, addressing the complex technical problem of verifying a ceiling on nuclear warheads.[16] The USSR is also prepared to adjust its negotiating stance to take into account American plans to maintain an air-based nuclear deterrent in Europe. Soviet analysts propose an initial deal on land-based systems followed by future limits on aircraft which would be synchronized with the CFE process.[17]

STRATEGIC ARMS CUTS

The dramatic change in the Soviet position on strategic arms reduction was due primarily to heightened Soviet interest in strengthening strategic stability. The Gorbachev leadership showed a willingness to cut substantially nuclear stockpiles, to place constraints on warheads, and to restructure Soviet forces. The Soviet concessions were intended to render the strategic environment safer for both sides. In particular, control of warhead proliferation, reduction of the destructive yield of arsenals, and cuts in fixed-site land-based missiles lowered each side's capacity and incentive for preemption. The issue on which the USSR was most reluctant to compromise—cruise missiles—also reflected the Soviet concern for stability. The accuracy and elusiveness to detection of cruise missiles were regarded as a threat to the Soviet second-strike potential.

The Strategic Arms Reduction Talks made little headway before 1985. Neither side seemed particularly interested in achieving progress, and the USSR had linked START to INF, refusing to cut its strategic arsenal unless NATO plans to deploy new missiles in Europe were abandoned. When the Soviet delegation walked out of the INF negotiations, START broke down as well. The Soviet START proposal of 1982 envisaged modest reductions in the ceilings set by SALT II,[18] a freeze on forward-based systems (FBS), and a ban on all cruise missiles with ranges greater than 600 kilometers. The Soviet government stuck to its position until the talks collapsed. The only flexibility shown was readiness to sanction deployments of ALCMs, which had been permitted by the SALT II Treaty.

The Gorbachev leadership's first offer on START was presented to President Reagan in September 1985 by Shevardnadze. It did away with the SALT II framework, and instead reduced by 50 percent delivery vehicles capable of reaching the other side's territory, placed a ceiling of 6,000 on "nuclear charges," and limited the number of warheads on any given leg of the triad to 60 percent of the total. This offer initiated three important trends in the Soviet approach to strategic arms reduction. First, the USSR sought substantial cuts in strategic arsenals. The sizable reduction in nuclear stockpiles reflected the diminishing Soviet reliance, prescribed by new thinking, on military power and on nuclear arms in particular. It also represented the shift from quantity to quality in defense, from deploying large forces to producing fewer but better weapons.

The second trend set by the September 1985 START proposal was to reduce the portion of the Soviet nuclear arsenal placed on ICBMs and thus to make the Soviet force posture more like that of the United States. The limit on warheads of any one leg of the triad to 60 percent of the total was generous enough to preclude substantial restructuring of Soviet nuclear forces,[19] but it set the precedent for warhead subceilings on different legs of the triad. Subsequent proposals, such as the counting rules, would provide further incentives to lower Soviet dependence on ICBMs. Reduction in land-based missiles comprised part of the Soviet effort to limit the vulnerability of its strategic stockpile. The shift from preemption to retaliation dictated the need to render Soviet nuclear forces survivable. The high command welcomed the creation of a more balanced nuclear triad as a way to preserve its options should nuclear war break out while fulfilling the requirements of a second-strike doctrine. Civilian experts regarded force restructuring as a means for strengthening strategic stability. They supported 50 percent cuts in strategic arms affecting all legs of the triad in order to stop the development of counterforce potentials on both sides.[20]

Third, the USSR wanted to lower the ratio of warheads to launchers. The 1985 offer on START was the first Soviet one to place aggregate limits on warheads as well as on missiles. Controlling warhead proliferation set the stage for deMIRVing, for decreasing the warhead/launcher ratio. Soviet civilian strategists were determined to initiate a process of deMIRVing in order to lessen the incentive to strike first and thereby to enhance stability. The military leadership was less keen on cutting warheads, since this would weaken the Soviet capacity to use its nuclear weapons against enemy military forces.

The Soviet stance on START underwent the next important shift in October 1986 at the Reykjavik summit. The USSR dropped its demand to count missiles and aircraft within range of the other side's homeland, namely, American FBSs, and instead proposed a 50 percent cut in strategic offensive arms. The inclusion of FBSs would have required greater reductions on the American side and so was bound to remain unacceptable to the United States. FBSs could, in any case, be incorporated into other negotiations. The ISRM Treaty banned all U.S. missiles in Europe capable of hitting Soviet territory. Medium-range aircraft escaped restriction until President Bush consented to put them on the table of the CFE talks. At Reykjavik, the superpowers agreed to aggregate ceilings on strategic nuclear delivery vehicles (SNDVs) of 1,600 and on warheads of 6,000, and to bomber counting rules whereby planes equipped only with nuclear gravity bombs and short-range attack missiles would count as one delivery vehicle against the 1,600 total and as one warhead against the 6,000 limit.

The counting rules took into consideration the relative ineffectiveness of aviation. Bombers enjoyed much less assurance of penetrating enemy defenses than missiles (including ALCMs) because they were liable to interception.

The counting rules encouraged greater reliance on strategic aviation, allowing the USSR to offset cuts in ICBMs with bombers rather than submarines. While the portion of the Soviet nuclear arsenal consisting of aviation grew, the relative size of the sea leg of the triad remained the same. The strongest constituency for nuclear submarines, aside from the Soviet navy, was found among civilian arms control experts who had less influence over force postures than the Ministry of Defense. Military officials staunchly supported the increased emphasis on air-based systems, which provided the flexibility to maintain a counterforce capability while conforming to the retaliatory strike doctrine.

At the Reykjavik summit, Gorbachev also accepted the principle of large reductions in heavy ICBMs, which meant decreasing the number of SS-18 missiles. The Soviet draft START treaty of July 1987 incorporated a 50 percent cut in heavy ICBMs, which the USSR in September agreed to express in terms of warheads (1,540 on 154 missiles). Soviet willingness to diminish its force of SS-18s is consistent with the no-first-use policy. Heavy ICBMs are best suited to preemption. Their reduction lowers the vulnerability of the Soviet arsenal and thus the incentive of each side to strike first. The START Treaty further strengthens strategic stability by banning the introduction of new heavy missiles. The Soviet concession on SS-18s, which are regarded by the United States as the most threatening component of Soviet nuclear forces, placated grave U.S. concerns and thereby raised American interest in concluding an accord on strategic arms reduction.

In its desire to render nuclear forces survivable, the Soviet delegation, throughout the Nuclear and Space Talks, remained adamant that mobile ICBMs should be allowed. The July 1987 draft START treaty presented by the USSR permitted mobile missiles. The Reagan administration opposed the Soviet position, but President Bush, who approved the development of both the

Midgetman missile and a rail system for the MX, accepted deployments of mobile ICBMs.

The Soviet Union agreed to sanction deployment of long-range nuclear-armed SLCMs (sea-launched cruise missiles). The Soviet side at the Reykjavik summit wanted to allow SLCMs on submarines but to ban their deployment on surface ships. The July 1987 draft START treaty placed a limit of 400 on SLCMs and permitted their basing only on submarines. At the December 1987 Washington summit, the USSR reluctantly conceded to the American suggestion of excluding SLCMs from the aggregate ceilings of 1,600 SNDVs and 6,000 warheads, but reaffirmed its intention of restricting SLCM deployments. This issue presented a major stumbling block in START negotiations until Secretary of State Baker's visit to Moscow in February 1990, when the sides agreed to take a "declaratory approach" to SLCMs whereby each side would state publicly the limits it was placing on sea-launched cruise missiles. The sides finally struck a relatively balanced deal in May. The United States consented to exclude ceilings on short-range SLCMs (300-600 km), of which it had none, and in return, the USSR dropped demands for verification measures that the U.S. navy opposed. Deployments of long-range SLCMs (over 600 km), which will not exceed 880, will be limited outside of the START Treaty through "politically binding" declarations.[21] Some Soviet officials expected more stringent restrictions to be placed on SLCMs. Shevardnadze replied to his critics that he had to compromise with the United States and that the absence of agreement would be dangerous because it would leave SLCM deployments completely unconstrained.[22]

The Soviet Union wanted to restrict SLCMs, which represented restricting a significantly new technological development in the arms race, as far as possible. The community of civilian strategists considered cruise missiles destabilizing because their accuracy and ability to elude radar detection placed Soviet retaliatory forces at risk. Soviet sea-based missiles were under less stringent control than were land-based weapons and thus presented a greater danger of unsanctioned nuclear use. Defense Ministry officials saw no need for nuclear-armed SLCMs and were reluctant to allow SLCM deployments until the development of Soviet SLCMs was nearing completion.

The USSR proved responsive to U.S. concerns about the destructive potential of its nuclear arsenal. Shevardnadze reported in September 1987 that the Soviet START package would reduce throw-weight by 50 percent, and in December, Gorbachev agreed to record the reduction in a mutually satisfactory manner. This concession reflected the Soviet move to a second-strike doctrine. Moreover, it coincided with the planned restructuring of the Soviet forces. The throw-weight of the Soviet stockpile would be cut in half during the process of reductions in SNDVs and warheads, especially in heavy ICBMs, and of shifting reliance from land-based missiles to bomber forces. The diminished destructive potential of Soviet forces would be partially offset by increased accuracy of Soviet nuclear weapons.

In October 1987, Gorbachev proposed warhead subceilings for the different legs of the triad: 3,000-3,300 on ICBMs; 1,800-2,000 on SLBMs; and 800-900 on ALCMs. The sides agreed in December to a limit of 4,900 warheads on ballistic missiles but remained in dispute over other subceilings. The USSR refused to include in START a 3,300 sublimit on ICBM warheads, because the United States rejected an equal ceiling on SLBM warheads. Shevardnadze turned down a U.S. proposal for a ban on MIRVed mobile ICBMs leading to the eventual elimination of all multiple warhead land-based missiles. He insisted that any restrictions on MIRVed ICBMs be accompanied by limits on sea-based ballistic missiles.[23] Nevertheless, at the June 1990 Washington summit, the sides set a limit of 1,100 warheads on mobile ICBMs. The Soviet Union could comfortably observe this ceiling, since it had decided to curtail production of rail-mobile SS-24s.[24]

ALCM counting rules generated considerable disagreement. The United States wanted to attribute 10 ALCMs to each heavy bomber, while the USSR preferred to count 20 to 22 ALCMs per bomber. Though more forthcoming on ALCMs than SLCMs, the Soviet Union sought to prevent a surge in cruise missile deployments that would noticeably enhance U.S. military capabilities. Differences over cruise missiles were finally resolved at the May 1990 ministerial meeting in Moscow. The United States made concessions to meet the Soviet position half way. It agreed to include in START all nuclear-armed ALCMs with ranges greater than 600 kilometers. A complicated formula for ALCM counting was worked out, which allows the United States to deploy more missiles and the Soviet Union to field more ALCM bombers.[25]

The START Treaty allows modernization programs on both sides to proceed more or less as planned. It places no significant constraints on deployments of the latest generation of nuclear arms. Soviet experts appeared dissatisfied with the meager qualitative restrictions imposed by START,[26] so they are likely, in future negotiations, to press for greater curbs on the technological improvement of nuclear forces.[27] They have put forward suggestions to place direct limits on new weapon systems, to lower warhead subceilings on the most powerful counterforce arms, and to permit only deployments of missiles with few MIRVs.[28] The USSR might well trade the elimination of Soviet SS-24s for a ban on MX missiles[29] or resuscitate its proposal to ban the introduction of new types of nuclear arms.

Soviet nuclear strategy is not affected much by the START accord. The USSR retains enough weapons to employ them against U.S. military assets. Arms cuts after START will exacerbate disagreements among Soviet experts over force structures by limiting the choice over preferred weapon systems. More important, they will begin to constrain Soviet counterforce capabilities and thus face resistance from the high command. The main impediment to deep reductions in strategic stockpiles lies in the Soviet military's adherence to counterforce targeting. Soviet progress toward minimum deterrence requires a political decision to reorient the present nuclear strategy away from counterforce targeting to a deterrent aimed primarily at destroying an aggressor's life centers.

The START Treaty decreases the actual warhead totals by about one-third. Both the Soviet Union and the United States are eager to make more cuts and to increase stability. The joint statement released at the June 1990 Washington summit contained a commitment to begin negotiations, upon the conclusion of START, to achieve further reductions in strategic arms. The talks will pursue the aim of enhancing strategic stability by removing incentives for a first strike, decreasing the concentration of warheads on delivery vehicles, and giving priority to survivable weapon systems.

CONTROL OF SPACE WEAPONS

Soviet compromise on strategic arms reduction was designed in part to raise American interest in an offense-defense trade-off. The USSR offered attractive concessions on START in an effort to entice the United States to limit the Strategic Defense Initiative. The Gorbachev leadership adamantly refused to sanction the development or deployment of space weapons. It modified its position to a small extent but stood firm on the fundamental issue. The Soviet government was resolved to prevent a race in ballistic missile defense, which was bound to prove costly and destabilizing. The expense of responding to deployment of SDI would drain resources needed for pressing military and civilian purposes. American BMD threatened to downgrade severely the USSR's retaliatory capability and thereby to encourage reckless U.S. behavior. Introduction of Soviet countermeasures would likely spark a competition in both offensive and defensive systems that would destabilize the strategic environment and undermine progress toward East-West cooperation.

The Soviet Union tried its best to maintain a link between offensive and defensive arms and to limit the scope of research, testing, and development of space weapons. The USSR consistently tied agreement on strategic arms reduction to observance of the ABM Treaty. It abandoned attempts to secure from the United States a legal commitment to uphold the treaty, but maintained the right to abrogate the START accord if American introduction of BMD went ahead. The failure to achieve agreement on space weapons left the issue unresolved. The USSR postponed the conclusion of a treaty limiting SDI but persists in its efforts to prevent by less formal methods the development and deployment of U.S. defensive weapons. Negotiations will continue on ABM Treaty interpretation to define permitted and prohibited activities related to SDI.

The USSR demanded a complete ban on Reagan's Strategic Defense Initiative until May 1986, and then, altering its stance, proposed an accord restricting SDI to the laboratory and committing both sides to observe the Anti-Ballistic Missile Treaty for fifteen to twenty years. At the Reykjavik summit, the suggested nonwithdrawal period was reduced to ten years. Ambiguities in the ABM Treaty, combined with the ambitious goals Reagan set for SDI, gave rise to serious disagreement over the existing limitations on the development of space-based defenses. The Soviet Union stuck to a narrow interpretation of the ABM Treaty that would greatly restrict the SDI program. The Reagan administration put forward a broad interpretation allowing development of most ABM systems and components, especially those derived from exotic technologies such as lasers.[30] Reconciling these two opposing viewpoints represented the main focus of negotiations on space weapons.

In the hope of settling the issue, Gorbachev proposed in January 1987 that a list of permissible areas of research on SDI be drawn up. The following month, he loosened the connection between offensive and defensive arms control. Dropping his insistence on linking a START agreement to a "strengthening" of the ABM Treaty, Gorbachev was prepared to make the START Treaty contingent upon a commitment to prevent deployment of weapons in space. In April 1987 the Soviet government expressed willingness to allow ABM-related activity as long as it occurred on earth, and in September made the further concession of accepting some testing in space.

The communiqué issued at the end of the December 1987 Washington summit passed over Soviet-American differences. The two sides declared their intention of concluding an accord to observe the ABM Treaty "as signed in 1972," which, to the USSR, implied the strict interpretation and to the United States, the broad understanding. Gorbachev also conceded that after this accord expired, "each side [would] be free to decide its course of action." The U.S. government took this phrase to mean that it would be permitted to deploy SDI after the period of nonwithdrawal from the ABM Treaty, but Soviet officials insisted that the proposed nonwithdrawal commitment simply reinforced the unlimited duration of the ABM Treaty and that they were not granting the United States the right to terminate the ABM Treaty at the end of this period.

The Soviet Union weakened the START-ABM link even further at the Moscow summit in June 1988. The joint statement released after the meeting committed the sides to reach a "separate" agreement on the ABM Treaty. The issue was finally resolved at Shevardnadze's encounter in September 1989 with James Baker in Wyoming. The Soviet side dropped its insistence on a nonwithdrawal pledge and thereby opened the way for signing a START Treaty without reaching agreement on space defenses. The dispute over ABM Treaty interpretation was thus left standing. The United States agreed to continue abiding by the ABM Treaty and was warned that abrogation of the treaty would provide grounds for the USSR to withdraw from the Strategic Arms Reduction Treaty. Shevardnadze remarked that U.S. violation of the traditional interpretation of the ABM Treaty would free the Soviet Union from its obligations under START. The Soviet side accepts research and certain testing conducted in space except for testing of ABM systems or components. At the Wyoming meeting, Shevardnadze announced the Soviet decision to dismantle completely the Krasnoyarsk radar, which Western observers considered a clear violation of the ABM Treaty, to demonstrate Soviet seriousness about averting competition in ballistic missile defenses.

The Nuclear and Space Talks will remain in session to discuss predictability measures and to clarify specifics of ABM Treaty interpretation. The joint statement issued at the June 1990 Washington summit instructs negotiators to discuss the relationship between strategic offensive and defensive arms, taking into account stabilizing reductions in offensive forces and development of new technologies. Nuclear and Space Talks will retain a loose link between START and SDI as it determines how ambiguities in the ABM Treaty apply to the latest space weapon technologies.

The Gorbachev leadership modified its stance on space weapons in order to facilitate agreement on strategic arms reduction. Failure to reach a START accord would block improvement in the strategic situation and cause enmity with the United States leading to intensified arms competition. In contrast, Soviet compromise stimulated progress in disarmament and complicated plans of U.S. conservatives to prepare for deployment of BMD. The Gorbachev leadership conceded relatively minor points to make sure it got its way on the central issues. It gave up attempts to attain legally binding assurances that the ABM Treaty would remain in force but let the United States know that breakout from the treaty would jeopardize the future of START. Once strategic weapons cuts were taking place, the United States would find great difficulty derailing the arms control process. Similarly, the USSR permitted some testing in space but stood firm against development and deployment of SDI. With the Soviet Union more forthcoming on BMD, the United States was in less of a position to ignore Soviet concerns. American options were further restricted by ongoing negotiations to draw up a list of permitted and prohibited SDI-related activities.

The Soviet stance on SDI ran parallel to majority opinion in the U.S. Congress. The American legislature generally supported SDI, appropriating increased funding for the program, but showed concern about the scope of SDI. Congressional opposition to the broad interpretation of the ABM Treaty kept work on the SDI program confined to the strict understanding of the treaty, and Senate ratification of the START Treaty could well be used to reaffirm the traditional interpretation of the ABM Treaty. Moreover, budgetary constraints virtually assured that the United

States could not afford to deploy SDI. Gorbachev and his supporters thus judged efforts to halt SDI entirely to be futile, so they concentrated attention on limiting the scope of SDI, in particular on preventing the program from reaching the developmental stage. By staking a position similar to that of Congress, they enjoyed greater chance of achieving their aims. Charging against the political tide of the United States would prove counterproductive. Flowing with the tide, and diverting it to less threatening areas, offered tangible benefits.

The Gorbachev leadership was encouraged to make concessions on space weapons by enhanced confidence in its ability to cope with the consequences of U.S. BMD deployments. Soviet scientists had concluded that a comprehensive space-based defense system would be ineffective and that even though more limited defenses were possible, a wide spectrum of accessible and relatively cheap countermeasures was available. The certainty that a race in BMD would prove very costly to the United States increased Soviet willingness to compromise on SDI.

The Gorbachev leadership, in contrast to its predecessors, took the initiative throughout most of the arms talks. It readily compromised in areas of Soviet advantage to demonstrate its commitment to conclude accords. It sustained momentum in the negotiations to persuade skeptics that arms agreements could be reached and thereby to consolidate domestic support for its policy of opening up to the West. Gorbachev and his advisors developed Soviet positions in stages, gaining the backing for one large concession before building a consensus for another. First they approved the principle of asymmetrical cuts, accepting equal ceilings on IRMs by excluding British and French forces, and then, nine months later, embraced the zero option for Europe. They kept the negotiation process moving to secure growing U.S. collaboration in reducing and restructuring nuclear arsenals. The Gorbachev leadership concentrated its efforts on forging progress in disarmament, designed proposals to which the United States could agree, and played down contentious issues that threatened to bring the arms talks to a standstill.

By its second year in office, the Gorbachev leadership had abandoned unproductive tactics in favor of a constructive approach. Public relations stunts, such as the April 1985 moratorium on SS-20 deployments and the plan to rid the world of nuclear weapons by the year 2000, may have generated some sympathy for the USSR but gave Western governments little indication of serious Soviet interest in arms control. Subsequent Soviet initiatives, though unveiled with great fanfare, contained substance for discussion. Gorbachev and his supporters shifted attention from issues having the greatest impact on Soviet security to those most easily resolved. They initially refused to compromise until the Reagan administration relented on SDI, but when negotiations stalled, they removed the link between European missiles and SDI and granted precedence to reaching an agreement on IRMs. Instead of trying to block U.S. weapon programs head on, Gorbachev and fellow reformers showed flexibility. They preserved the basic Soviet stance, for instance, on slowing down the technological arms race, but offered small concessions to the United States (giving consent to SLCM limits outside of the START Treaty) or proposed new avenues to explore (such as the list to settle differences over ABM Treaty interpretation).

The Soviet Union under Gorbachev exhibited sensitivity to Western interests and framed initiatives to form the basis for agreement. It dropped demands, for example, to include forward-based systems in START and third-party forces in INF, that the West considered unreasonable. It compromised in order to satisfy particular U.S. concerns. The generous bomber counting rule avoided excessive constraints on strategic aviation. The second zero prevented the USSR from increasing its superiority in SRMs. American proposals, including the zero option, warhead ceilings, limits on throw-weight, and reduction of (and ban on new) heavy ICBMs, were incorporated into Soviet draft treaties. The Soviet Union responded positively to changes in the U.S. stance. After NATO declared its readiness to cut TNWs, the USSR shifted emphasis from elimination to gradual reduction of tactical arms. The justifications of Gorbachev and Shevardnadze for various Soviet concessions reflected the belief that placing some restraints on U.S. weapon programs was preferable to having none.

The Gorbachev leadership stood firm when vital Soviet interests were at stake. In certain cases the United States came around to the Soviet position, for instance, to sanction deployments of mobile ICBMs. On other issues, disagreements were too contentious to resolve at the time and were set aside. Significant qualitative restrictions in strategic arms and an accord reconfirming the validity of the ABM Treaty will await changes in U.S. policy and further negotiation.

NOTES

1. *Izvestia*, 26 November 1983.
2. "Protsess Ratifikatsy Dogovora po RSD-RMD Nachalsya" ["The Process of Ratifying the ISRM Treaty has Begun"], *Vestnik Ministerstva Inostrannykh Del* [*Bulletin of the Ministry of Foreign Affairs*], *(MID)*, no. 4, 1988, p. 17.
3. "Dogovor po RSD-RMD: Protsess Ratifikatsy" ["ISRM Treaty: The Ratification Process"], *Vestnik MID*, no. 5, 1988, p. 17.
4. "Protsess Ratifikatsy," p. 17.
5. *Pravda*, 17 September 1987.
6. *Izvestia*, 29 May 1988.
7. "Dogovor po RSD-RMD," p. 16.
8. "Protsess Ratifikatsy," p. 17.
9. *Pravda*, 12 June 1986.
10. Gorbachev in *Pravda*, 12 July 1988.
11. *Pravda*, 14 May 1989.
12. Pavel Bayev, Vitali Zhurkin, Sergei Karaganov and Viktor Shein, *Tactical Nuclear Weapons in Europe* (Moscow: Novosti, 1990), pp. 43–44.
13. Ibid.
14. Sergei V. Kortunov, "Vozmozhny li Peregovory po Takticheskomu Yadernomu Oruzhiyu?" ["Are Negotiations on Tactical Nuclear Weapons Possible?"], *MEMO*, February 1990, pp. 32, 39.
15. Gorbachev promised to undertake unilateral reductions in Soviet TNWs once NATO was disposed to start talks, *Pravda*, 7 July 1989. At the June 1990 CSCE Conference in Copenhagen, Shevardnadze declared that the USSR would pull 60 tactical missile launchers, 250 nuclear artillery pieces and 1,500 nuclear warheads out of Eastern Europe. This represents a

reduction of one-third of the Soviet tactical missiles deployed outside the Soviet border and a 46 percent cut in Soviet nuclear artillery tubes, according to Lee Feinstein, "Soviet Union to Reduce Short-Range Nuclear Weapons," *Arms Control Today*, vol. 20, no. 5, June 1990, p. 33.

16. Bayev et al., *Tactical Nuclear Weapons in Europe*, pp. 43–45.

17. Ibid. Dual-capable strike aircraft are included in CFE but their nuclear charges are not.

18. The Soviet START proposal lowered the aggregate limit on strategic nuclear delivery vehicles from 2,250 to 1,800, the subceiling on MIRVed missiles plus ALCMs from 1,320 to 1,200, on MIRVed missiles from 1,200 to 1,080, and on MIRVed ICBMs from 820 to 680.

19. The USSR at the time had 6,420 ICBM warheads out of a total of 9,887 (see *Military Balance 1985/86*), p. 180, amounting to 64 percent.

20. A. G. Arbatov, A. A. Vasilyev, and A. A. Kokoshin, "Yadernoye Oruzhiye i Strategicheskaya Stabilnost" ["Nuclear Weaponry and Strategic Stability"], *SShA*, October 1987, pp. 20–21.

21. The sides will make annual "politically binding" declarations of the maximum number of long-range nuclear-armed SLCMs to be deployed in each of the following five years. The number will not exceed 880. The sides will annually exchange confidential data on SLCMs with a range of 300-600 kilometers.

22. Interviewed in *New Times*, no. 18 (May), 1990, p. 36.

23. Dunbar Lockwood, "START Talks Falter, Early Summit Scheduled," *Arms Control Today*, vol. 20, no. 4, May 1990, p. 25.

24. Soviet officials disclosed that deployments of rail-mobile SS-24s will stop once their number has reached 36, as reported by the *Washington Post*, 3 August 1990.

25. U.S. bombers may be loaded with up to 20 ALCMs, Soviet bombers with up to 12. Against the 6,000 aggregate warhead limit, each of the first 150 U.S. bombers will count as carrying 10 ALCMs, and each additional bomber will be attributed with the actual number of ALCMs for which it is equipped. The first 210 Soviet bombers will count as carrying 8 ALCMs each, and each additional bomber will be attributed with the actual number of ALCMs for which it is equipped.

26. Andrei Kortunov and Sergei Fedorenko, "After the Treaty: What's in Store?" *New Times*, no. 16 (April), 1990, p. 10. The START Treaty bans new heavy ICBMs and SLBMs, ballistic missiles with more than ten warheads, MIRVed ALCMs, and flight testing and deployment of existing types of ICBMs and SLBMs with more warheads than agreed at the December 1987 Washington summit.

27. Sergei V. Kortunov, "Stability in the Nuclear World," *International Affairs*, March 1990, pp. 10–11.

28. Alexei G. Arbatov, "START: Good, Bad or Neutral?" *Survival*, vol. 31, no. 4, July/August 1989, pp. 295–96.

29. Nikolai Chervov, head of the General Staff's arms control department, in *Washington Post*, 21 January 1990.

30. For details see Alan B. Sherr, *The Other Side of Arms Control* (Boston: Unwin Hyman, 1988), pp. 220–25.

7

CONCLUSION

Change in the USSR's policy on nuclear disarmament is driven by the Gorbachev leadership's determination to modernize the Soviet system. Gorbachev has guided the process, garnering the political support needed to transform the sources and exercise of Soviet power. Economic restructuring claims increasing industrial capacity and technological resources from the defense complex and requires growing Soviet involvement in the global economy. New thinking supplants Soviet reliance on military might with the building of economic strength through domestic reform and East-West cooperation. Stability takes precedence over military effectiveness when designing Soviet nuclear forces. More and more, weapons rivalry is replaced by joint efforts to reconfigure the nuclear balance, and superpower relations are characterized by constructive interaction in the political, economic, and social spheres. While recognizing the durability of transatlantic ties, the Soviet Union promotes the establishment of new European security arrangements that foster a gradual fusion of the two halves of the continent.

Disarmament advances Soviet participation in the international system by removing barriers to Soviet entry and overcoming resistance at home. It draws Western collaboration to restructure nuclear arsenals, ensuring that Soviet arms cuts are reciprocated and that rough parity is maintained. It provides an effective method of decreasing the defense burden while enhancing stability. Accords with the United States reduce or eliminate weapon systems, such as multiwarhead ICBMs and intermediate-range missiles, which endanger Soviet retaliatory capabilities. The easing of Western military pressure on the USSR and the savings resulting from cuts in the Soviet nuclear stockpile generate domestic approval of arms control and of the Gorbachev leadership's endeavor to reconstruct the Soviet system.

As their tenure progressed, Gorbachev and his advisors accorded diminishing priority to nuclear disarmament because it served more to initiate than to press forward change in Soviet security policy. Reduction of nuclear arms was the most immediate way to relieve the Western threat and to decrease the military component of Soviet power. When military competition with the United States and Western Europe slackened, other foreign and domestic aspects of the reform process grew in importance. By 1990, the USSR was primarily concerned with the conditions for German unification, the struggle of Soviet republics for sovereignty or independence, with attaining Western economic cooperation and assistance, and utilizing the savings from defense cuts to boost civilian production.

The prospects for rebuilding the Soviet system are contingent upon nuclear disarmament to an ever lesser degree. The Gorbachev leadership's arms control policy has helped to subdue resistance to reductions in Soviet military expenditures and to furnish the USSR with entry into the global economy and international system. The fact that Western willingness to lend assistance to Soviet restructuring appeared sooner than the Soviet economy could absorb the full benefits of it provides an indication of both the success of Gorbachev's approach to arms control and the limits of disarmament's contribution to his overall aims. Nuclear weapons cuts can promote further decreases in defense spending and enhancement of East-West cooperation, but must increasingly be complemented and replaced by other means to stimulate economic growth and to widen Soviet participation in world developments.

The future direction of Soviet arms control policy will be determined by the leadership's resolve to master the technological revolution. Weakening the commitment to modernize the Soviet system could stall or reverse progress in the USSR's pursuit of disarmament. Even without a change of president, the leadership could slacken its reform efforts, neglecting to implement new legislation and allowing traditional Soviet patterns of government administration and economic management to reemerge. For instance, the defense complex could retain its virtual monopoly of high technology resources and, by expanding its civilian production under a system of state orders, remain a large centrally planned part of the economy. Retrenchment on reform would undermine the basis of the revised national security aims. Soviet economic development would grow more autarkic, and the resulting reduction in the need for Western cooperation would erode Soviet interest in collaborating with the West to enhance stability. Conceivably, economic growth and efficiency could again be subordinated to the exercise of military might and to attempts to keep the Soviet empire intact.

Far more likely, the process of transforming the USSR will continue and intensify. Gorbachev is securely in power and is dedicated to bringing reform to fruition. His lack of success so far has depreciated the authority of his leadership, but in the absence of credible alternative programs, poor economic performance does less to discredit than to encourage restructuring. Gorbachev has gained enough experience and dominance over conservative rivals to begin pushing the Communist Party to the margins of society and introducing a market economy. If he proves incapable of making the painful adjustments required to revitalize the Soviet system, his goals might be realized by a successor who not only controls the levers of power in Moscow but also commands legitimacy in the country at large.

Further elaboration of internal and external policies is needed to advance the Soviet position on arms control. Greater civilian input in formulating defense policy and progress in military reform would spur disarmament. Publication of a detailed defense budget, even though misleading in the absence of price reform, would prompt public debate on specific military postures and strategies. The Supreme Soviet would strengthen its authority if the Defense Committee held open hearings on arms procurement to assess the merits and cost of each new weapons system. Augmenting the institutional control over defense policy by civilians would contribute to the restructuring of military industry. The Soviet government plans to provide investments for conversion and then to leave defense firms to fend for themselves. Defense contracts would be awarded on a competitive basis, and the remaining output of military plants would be sold in free markets. Firms would keep their earnings, but if they proved inefficient, they would go bankrupt. As they shift production to consumer goods, authority over them could be assumed by civilian ministries to prepare them for privatization. If the Gorbachev leadership carries through its plans to reform the defense complex, the resulting immediate-term disruption in output of weaponry will intensify the pressure on the USSR to proceed with disarmament.

Continued arms reductions require additional adjustments in Soviet foreign and defense policies. A broader acceptance of new thinking—granting precedence to economic modernization, overcoming skepticism about Western intentions and the benefits of arms control, and giving preference to diplomacy over military might in protecting Soviet interests—would help the USSR to define more precisely its world role in the face of its declining global influence. Further revision of Soviet nuclear strategy, in particular altering targeting priorities, would enhance stability at the expense of war-fighting capabilities. The Soviet Union can enter more nuclear arms agreements if it develops with the United States a better mutual understanding of strategic stability and builds solid institutions for security cooperation with members of the Atlantic alliance.

Soviet opposition to large-scale antiballistic missile defenses will most likely persist since the USSR is determined to maintain an effective second-strike capability and to avoid a costly and dangerous race in defensive systems and offensive countermeasures. While pursuing negotiations to define which SDI-related activities should be prohibited or permitted, the USSR faces the task of satisfying some American demands but reaffirming its fundamental position. The Soviet Union will probably undertake further reductions in offensive forces so long as the consensus in Washington remains critical of the development and deployment of space weapons. As strategic arms are lowered to minimum levels, the USSR expects to reach some agreement with the United States on the precise parameters of the SDI program and eventually to attain a firm legal commitment banning the introduction of new ballistic missile defenses.

The START Treaty reduces nuclear stockpiles by roughly one-third and preserves substantial counterforce capabilities distributed fairly evenly among the three legs of the nuclear triads. The Soviet and U.S. presidents have expressed the intention of seeking deeper cuts, decreasing the concentration of warheads on delivery vehicles, and strengthening the survivability of nuclear arsenals. Talks to put these principles into practice will encounter difficulties in curbing qualitative improvements in weaponry and selecting which retaliatory systems to retain. The USSR will need not only to reach an understanding with the United States on deploying similar weapons or balancing different ones, but also to settle disagreements among Soviet experts on force postures, to choose the right mix of SLBMs and mobile ICBMs, and to decide whether to maintain a strong bomber force or simply concentrate on single warhead missiles. Moreover, negotiations will be complicated by Soviet targeting policy. As arms cuts go deeper, counterforce potential is eroded, and Soviet nuclear strategy must increasingly be reoriented to destroy only industrial and population centers. Soviet targeting plans must be changed entirely in order to reach minimum levels of deterrence.

Further strategic arms reductions will encourage cuts in the nuclear stockpiles remaining in Europe, particularly the U.S. forward-based systems and the British and French forces. NATO's justification for retaining tactical nuclear weapons is being rapidly undermined by German unification, conventional arms cuts, and the disintegration of the Warsaw Pact. U.S. nuclear engagement is gradually being superseded by the formation of pan-European security structures. Minimum deterrence can be achieved in a couple of years, but the elimination of U.S. nuclear weapons in Europe will only be possible once the new security arrangements are both comprehensive enough to fulfill Soviet needs and sufficiently solid and coherent for Western Europe to manage without U.S. nuclear guarantees.

A persistent Soviet drive to create a vibrant and technologically mature economy would confirm the overriding importance that the Soviet leadership attaches to domestic renewal and would thereby allow the Soviet Union to watch its superpower status dissipate without growing alarmed. Evidence that the reform program will endure would persuade the West to embrace the USSR as a full participant in the international community, to extend assistance to Soviet restructuring, and to work more closely in settling differences and solving common problems. Increasing collaboration on security issues, particularly joint efforts to reduce and reconfigure the nuclear balance, will stimulate future progress in nuclear disarmament.

GLOSSARY

ABM: antiballistic missile

ALCM: air-launched cruise missile

BMD: ballistic missile defense

C^3: command, control, and communications

CFE: Conventional Forces in Europe

FBS: forward-based systems

GLCM: ground-launched cruise missile

ICBM: intercontinental ballistic missile

IMEMO: Institute of World Economy and International Relations

INF: Intermediate-range Nuclear Forces

IRM: intermediate-range missile (1,000–5,500 km)

ISRM: intermediate- and short-range missiles

MIRV: multiple independently targeted reentry vehicle

NST: Nuclear and Space Talks

SALT: Strategic Arms Limitation Treaty

SDI: Strategic Defense Initiative

SLBM: submarine-launched ballistic missile

SLCM: sea-launched cruise missile

SNVD: strategic nuclear delivery vehicle

SRM: short-range missile (500–1,000 km)

SSBN: nuclear-powered ballistic missile submarine

SS-NX-20: surface-to-surface, naval experimental, missile no. 20 (in the order that it was sighted by U.S. intelligence)

START: Strategic Arms Reduction Talks

TASM: tactical air-to-surface missile

Throw-weight: total weight of the ballistic missile components launched into space; includes warheads and the hardware needed to guide them to their targets after the initial stages of the missiles have fallen off

TNW: tactical nuclear weapons (less than 500 km)

SELECTED BIBLIOGRAPHY

BOOKS

Alford, Jonathon (ed.). *The Soviet Union: Security Policies and Constraints.* London: International Institute for Strategic Studies, 1985.

Becker, Abraham S. *Sitting on Bayonets.* Santa Monica, CA: RAND, December 1985.

Berman, Robert P., and John C. Baker. *Soviet Strategic Forces: Requirements and Responses.* Washington, DC: Brookings, 1982.

Bialer, Seweryn. *The Soviet Paradox.* New York: Knopf, 1986.

Blechman, Barry M., and Cathleen S. Fisher. *The Silent Partner: West Germany and Arms Control.* Cambridge, MA: Ballinger, 1988.

Brzezinski, Zbigniew. *The Grand Failure.* New York: Collier, 1990.

Garthoff, Raymond L. *Détente and Confrontation.* Washington, DC: Brookings, 1985.

Gelman, Harry. *Gorbachev's Policies toward Western Europe.* Santa Monica, CA: RAND, October 1987.

Gottemoeller, Rose E. *Conflict and Consensus in the Soviet Armed Forces.* Santa Monica, CA: RAND, October 1989.

Hasegawa, Tsuyoshi, and Alex Pravda (eds.). *Perestroika: Soviet Domestic and Foreign Policies.* London: Royal Institute of International Affairs, 1990.

Haslam, Jonathan. *The Soviet Union and the Politics of Nuclear Weapons in Europe, 1969–87.* London: Macmillan, 1989.

Herspring, Dale R. *The Soviet High Command 1967–1989.* Princeton, NJ: Princeton University Press, 1990.

Holloway, David. *The Soviet Union and the Arms Race.* New Haven, CT: Yale University Press, 1983.

Hudson, George E. (ed.). *Soviet National Security Policy under Perestroika.* Boston: Unwin Hyman, 1990.

Jacobsen, Carl G. (ed.). *Strategic Power USA/USSR*. New York: St. Martin's Press, 1990.
Laird, Robbin F., and Susan L. Clark (eds.). *The USSR and the Western Alliance*. Boston: Unwin Hyman, 1990.
Lynch, Allen. *Gorbachev's International Outlook: Intellectual Origins and Political Consequences*. New York: Institute for East-West Security Studies, 1989.
Malcolm, Neil. *Soviet Policy Perspectives on Western Europe*. London: Royal Institute of International Affairs, 1989.
Mandelbaum, Michael (ed.). *The Other Side of the Table*. New York: Council on Foreign Relations, 1990.
McGwire, Michael. *Military Objectives in Soviet Foreign Policy*. Washington, DC: Brookings, 1987.
Meyer, Stephen M. *Soviet Theater Nuclear Forces*. Adelphi Paper nos. 187 & 188. London: International Institute for Strategic Studies, Winter 1983/84.
Parrott, Bruce. *The Soviet Union and Ballistic Missile Defense*. Boulder, CO: Westview, 1987.
Scott, Harriet Fast, and William F. Scott. *The Armed Forces of the USSR*. 3rd ed. Boulder, CO: Westview, 1984.
Shenfield, Stephen. *The Nuclear Predicament*. London: Royal Institute of International Affairs, 1987.
Sherr, Alan B. *The Other Side of Arms Control*. Boston: Unwin Hyman, 1988.
Talbott, Strobe. *The Master of the Game*. New York: Knopf, 1988.
Valenta, Jiri, and William C. Potter. *Soviet Decisionmaking for National Security*. Boston: Allen & Unwin, 1984.
Warner, Edward L. *Soviet Concepts and Capabilities for Limited Nuclear War*. Santa Monica, CA: RAND, February 1989.

ARTICLES

Adomeit, Hannes. "Gorbachev and German Unification: Revision of Thinking, Realignment of Power." *Problems of Communism*, vol. 39, no. 4, July/August 1990.
Adranga, Steven P. "A New Soviet Military? Doctrine and Strategy." *Orbis*, vol. 33, no. 2, Spring 1989.
Bajusz, William D. and Lisa D. Shaw. "The Forthcoming 'SNF Negotiations'." *Survival*, vol. 32, no. 4, July/August 1990.
Bialer, Seweryn. " 'New Thinking' and Soviet Foreign Policy." *Survival*, vol. 30, no. 4, July/August 1988.

———. "The Passing of the Soviet Order?" *Survival*, vol. 32, no. 2, March/April 1990.
Breslauer, George W. "Evaluating Gorbachev as Leader." *Soviet Economy*, vol. 5, no. 4, October-December 1989.
Brown, Archie. "The Soviet Leadership and Struggle for Political Reform." *Harriman Institute Forum*, vol. 1, no. 4, April 1988.
———. "Political Change in the Soviet Union." *World Policy Journal*, vol. 6, no. 3, Summer 1989.
Currie, Kenneth. "Soviet General Staff's New Role." *Problems of Communism*, vol. 33, no. 2, March/April 1984.
Dawisha, Karen. "Perestroika, Glasnost and Soviet Foreign Policy." *Harriman Institute Forum*, vol. 3, no. 1, January 1990.
Evangelista, Matthew. "Economic Reform and Military Technology in Soviet Security Policy." *Harriman Institute Forum*, vol. 2, no. 1, January 1989.
Garthoff, Raymond L. "New Thinking in Soviet Military Doctrine." *Washington Quarterly*, vol. 11, no. 3, Summer 1988.
Goldberg, Andrew C. "Western Analysts Reappraise Soviet Strategic Policy." *Washington Quarterly*, vol. 12, no. 2, Spring 1989.
Goure, Daniel. "A New Soviet National Security Policy for the 21st Century." *Strategic Review*, vol. 16, no. 4, Fall 1989.
Goure, Leon. "A 'New' Soviet Military Doctrine: Reality or Mirage?" *Strategic Review*, vol. 15, no. 3, Summer 1988.
Hewett, Ed A. "*Perestroyka* and the Congress of People's Deputies." *Soviet Economy*, vol. 5, no. 1, January-March 1989.
Holloway, David. "Gorbachev's New Thinking." *Foreign Affairs*, America and the World, vol. 68, no. 1, 1988/89.
Horelick, Arnold L. "U.S.-Soviet Relations: Threshold of a New Era." *Foreign Affairs*, vol. 69, no. 1, America and the World 1989/90.
Hough, Jerry F. "Gorbachev Consolidating Power." *Problems of Communism*, vol. 36, no. 4, July/August 1987.
———. "Gorbachev's Politics." *Foreign Affairs*, vol. 68, no. 5, Winter 1989/90.
Kaufman, Richard F. "Causes of the Slowdown in Soviet Defense." *Soviet Economy*, vol. 1, no. 1, January-March 1985.
Kincade, William H., and T. Keith Thomson. "Economic Conversion in the USSR: Its Role in *Perestroyka*." *Problems of Communism*, vol. 39, no. 1, January/February 1990.
Lambeth, Benjamin, and Kevin Lewis. "The Kremlin and SDI." *Foreign Affairs*, vol. 67, no. 2, Spring 1988.
Larrabee, F. Stephen. "Gorbachev and the Soviet Military." *Foreign Affairs*, vol. 67, no. 3, Summer 1988.

_____. "Soviet Policy towards Germany: New Thinking and Old Realities." *Washington Quarterly*, vol. 12, no. 3, Summer 1989.

Legvold, Robert. "The Revolution in Soviet Foreign Policy." *Foreign Affairs*, vol. 68, no. 1, America and the World, 1988/89.

Lynch, Allen. "Does Gorbachev Matter Anymore?" *Foreign Affairs*, vol. 69, no. 3, Summer 1990.

Matosich, Andrew J., and Bonnie K. Matosich. "Machine Building: *Perestroyka*'s Sputtering Engine." *Soviet Economy*, vol. 4, no. 2, April-June 1988.

McConnell, James M. "SDI, the Soviet Investment Debate and Soviet Military Policy." *Strategic Review*, vol. 16, no. 1, Winter 1988.

Meyer, Stephen M. "The Sources and Prospects of Gorbachev's New Political Thinking on Security." *International Security*, vol. 13, no. 2, Fall 1988.

Odom, William E. "Soviet Military Doctrine." *Foreign Affairs*, vol. 67, no. 5, Winter 1988/89.

_____. "The Soviet Military in Transition." *Problems of Communism*, vol. 39, no. 3, May/June 1990.

Parrott, Bruce. "Soviet National Security under Gorbachev." *Problems of Communism*, vol. 37, no. 6, November/December 1988.

Petersen, Phillip A., and Notra Trulock. "A 'New' Soviet Military Doctrine: Origins and Implications." *Strategic Review*, vol. 15, no. 3, Summer 1988.

Puschel, Karen. "Can Moscow Live with SDI?" *Survival*, vol. 31, no. 1, January/February 1989.

Rice, Condoleezza. "The Party, the Military, and Decision Authority in the Soviet Union." *World Politics*, vol. 40, no. 1, October 1987.

Rivkin, David B. "The Soviet Approach to Nuclear Arms Control." *Survival*, vol. 29, no. 6, November/December 1987.

Sestanovich, Stephen. "Gorbachev's Foreign Policy: A Diplomacy of Decline," *Problems of Communism*, vol. 37, no. 1, January/February 1988.

_____. "Inventing the Soviet National Interest." *National Interest*, no. 20, Summer 1990.

Slocombe, Walter B. "Force Posture Consequences of the START Treaty." *Survival*, vol. 30, no. 5, September/October 1988.

Snyder, Jack. "Richness, Rigor, and Relevance in the Study of Soviet Foreign Policy." *International Security*, vol. 9, no. 3, Winter 1984/85.

_____. "Science and Sovietology: Bridging the Methods Gap in Soviet Foreign Policy Studies." *World Politics*, vol. 40, no. 2, January 1988.

Stent, Angela. "The Soviet Union and Western Europe: Divided Continent or Common House?" *Harriman Institute Forum*, vol. 2, no. 9, September 1989.

Teague, Elizabeth, and Dawn Mann. "Gorbachev's Dual Role." *Problems of Communism*, vol. 39, no. 1, January/February 1990.

Warner, Edward L. "New Thinking and Old Realities in Soviet Defense Policy." *Survival*, vol. 31, no. 1, January/February 1989.

Wettig, Gerhard. " 'New Thinking' on Security and East-West Relations." *Problems of Communism*, vol. 37, no. 2, March/April 1988.

INDEX

ABM (Anti-Ballistic Missile): competition, 79; cost, 108; countermeasures, 77–78; interest in, 78–79; opposition to, 76, 128, 162–63. *See also* BMD; space-based defenses

ABM Treaty, 78, 79, 107, 109–10, 115, 156; duration, 151–52; interpretation, 110, 112, 151–52, 153, 155; link to START, 15, 78, 150, 152, 153

Academy of Sciences, 20, 22, 24

air defense, 55, 86

Akhromeyev, Sergei, 18, 19, 60, 138, 140

ALCM (Air-Launched Cruise Missile), 85, 144, 148, 157 n.18, 26; counting rules, 146, 148–49, 157 n.25

Arbatov, Alexei, 55, 86, 87, 109; ABM, 78–79; command and control, 83; nuclear strategy, 81, 82; sufficiency, 58, 65

Arbatov, Georgi, 23, 101–102, 137

armed forces, 62, 63, 79; size, 5, 53, 55, 64; technological basis, 2, 4; restructuring of, 3, 11. *See also* military power; military high command

arms buildup, 4, 6, 54, 58, 68, 102

arms race, 65, 101; causes, 55, 57–58, 59; economic impact, 57–58, 62, 106; space defenses, 109, 153, 162–63; technological, 64, 135, 147, 155. *See also* BMD, competition

artillery, 88–89, 126, 142, 156–57 n.15

aviation. *See* bombers

Baker, James, 111, 147, 152

Belousov, Igor, 40

Blagovolin, Sergei, 54–55, 57

BMD (Ballistic Missile Defense): British and French concerns, 114; competition, 109, 150, 154; countermeasures, 78, 108; deployment, 75, 153; interest in, 78; link to offensive arms, 110, 163; retaliation, 77, 79; *See also* ABM; space-based defenses

Bogdanov, Radomir, 54, 59

bombers, 84, 86, 145, 163; counting rules, 145–146, 155, 157 n.25; modernization, 85, 89–90; tactical, 142, 143, 157 n.17
Bovin, Aleksandr, 51, 56, 61, 100, 113
Brezhnev, Leonid, 7; approach to arms control, 1–2; Doctrine, 53; global problems, 51; mistakes, 57, 59, 68, 101; mutual deterrence, 3, 76; nuclear parity in Europe, 117
Bush, George, 111–12, 124–25, 126, 145, 146–47
Bush administration, 111, 112, 121
Bykov, Oleg, 37, 39, 101, 110–11

capitalism, 49, 51, 52, 56, 68. *See also* imperialism
Carlucci, Frank, 105, 106
Central Committee, 20, 24; Commission on International Policy, 16–17; International Department, 16, 21
Central Committee Plenums: April 1985, 30; September 1988, 15
CFE (Conventional Forces in Europe), 92, 125, 126, 143, 157 n.17
CIA estimates: savings from START, 39; Soviet military expenditures, 34–35, 38
Chebrikov, Viktor, 14, 15
Chernenko, Konstantin, 49
civilian strategists, 66, 77, 83, 91, 145, 147; policy making, 24–26; targeting, 79, 81, 87; weapon systems, 81–82, 85–87. *See also* Arbatov, Alexei; Kokoshin; Zhurkin
class conflict, 49–50, 53

command and control, 83, 86, 92, 108
Common European Home, 10, 23, 120–21, 122, 131 n.57. *See also* European security system
Communist Party, 16, 161; Conference, 19th (June 1988), 20, 33, 41; Congress, 27th (February 1986), 48, 49; Congress, 28th (July 1990), 15, 17, 19, 20, 33; Revised Program (1986), 50, 62; Secretariat, 16. *See also* Central Committee; Politburo
concessions, 68, 127, 135, 154–56; resistance to, 14, 62, 67; space weapons, 154
Congress of People's Deputies, 16
conservatives, 11, 13, 55, 161. *See also* Gorbachev, opposition to; new political thinking
conventional force cuts, 8, 19–20, 39, 91, 125, 141
conventional strikes on nuclear assets, 89, 91
conventional war option, 6, 89, 91
conversion, 22, 29, 40–41
counterforce. *See* targeting
CSCE (Conference on Security and Disarmament in Europe), 24, 121

damage limitation, 80, 81
Dashichev, Vyacheslav, 58
Davydov, Yuri, 113–14, 118, 119, 122
decision making, 10, 11, 13, 14, 25
decline, 53, 54, 60, 64, 162
defense: political control, 19, 20, 25; qualitative parameters, 19, 41, 65, 144

defense budget, 22, 37, 39, 55, 161–62. *See also* defense burden; defense spending
defense burden, 3–4, 34–38, 65, 159–60. *See also* defense budget; defense spending
defense complex, 36, 38–43, 161. *See also* military reform
Defense Council, 13, 14, 19, 24, 75
Defense Ministry, 17, 20, 42, 146, 147–48
defense sector. *See* defense complex
defense spending, 37, 43, 54. *See also* defense budget; defense burden
détente, 61, 102, 103, 118
deterrence, 93; concept, 55, 77; extended, 117, 119, 120; minimum, 66, 127, 149, 163, 164
diplomacy, 47, 49, 60, 62, 68, 104. *See also* foreign policy
Dobrynin, Anatoli, 16, 24, 57
domestic reform: aims, 47, 48; economy, 29–34; international aspects, 3, 4, 13–14; prospects, 160–62; security interests, 60–61
dual-capable weapons, 92, 126, 143, 157 n.17

Eastern Europe, 52–53, 127; force withdrawals from 91, 125, 143, 156 n.15; revolutions, 53, 111, 120, 122
East-West cooperation, 3–4, 99, 102–103; arms control, 64, 68, 93; prospects, 160–61; resistance to, 53. *See also* United States, relations with USSR; Western Europe, cooperation with USSR

economic growth, 29–34, 50, 54, 160, 161
economic potential, 36, 48, 54, 57
economy, global, 3, 31–32, 48, 50–51, 64
escalation: conventional to nuclear, 87–88, 89, 91; dominance, 117, 140
European security system, 52, 113, 120–122; nuclear weapons, 119, 124–125, 127, 164

first strike: doctrine, 76; incentive, 146, 150; potential, 82, 135; by United States, 64, 65; weapons, 75–76
flexible response, 123, 126
force requirements, 25, 75, 86–87, 163
Foreign Ministry, 16, 20–21, 24, 119
foreign policy, 103, 162; reassessment, 100–102. *See also* diplomacy
FBS (Forward-Based Systems), 90, 144, 145, 155, 163
France, 114, 120, 125; nuclear weapons, 19, 88, 123–24, 136–39

Gareyev, Makhmut, 37, 89
General Staff, 18, 19, 24–25, 79–80, 81, 86
Germany, 114, 120, 124–25, 142; East, 141; unification, 15, 122–23, 160, 164
global interdependence, 51, 56
global problems, 51, 111
Gorbachev, Mikhail: aims, xi–xii, 2–4, 13–14; arms race, 57, 64; arms reductions in Europe, 87–88, 91; associates, 12–13; British and French nuclear forces,

123; capitalism, 56, 57; civilian experts, 24; collective leadership, 15, 17; Common European Home, 10; concessions, 135; conventional arms cuts, 125; decision making, 20, 25–26; defense industry, 41; disarmament proposals, 68; Eastern Europe, 52–53; East-West cooperation, 64, 99; economic reform, 30–34, 43; European security system, 121; future policy, 161–62; Germany, 122, 125; ISRM, 137–41; military establishment, 17–18; military expenditures, 35, 37; minimum deterrence, 66; negotiating tactics, 154–56; new political thinking, 47–49, 60, 61–62; nuclear disarmament, 1–2, 4, 93, 127, 159–60; nuclear strategy, 75, 79; nuclear weapons, 55; opposition to, 14–16, 53; personal contribution, 12, 14; personal staff, 16, 21; policy toward Western Europe, 112, 115–17, 122, 126; presidency, 17; SDI, 109, 150–54; speech to United Nations, 19–20, 55; START, 143–44, 146, 148; technological progress, 50; Third World, 52; U.S. presence in Europe, 115, 136; U.S.-Soviet relations, 102–106, 112
Great Britain, 114, 125; nuclear weapons, 19, 88, 123–24, 136–39
Gromov, Boris, 63
Gromyko, Andrei, 12, 14, 15, 20
GLCM (Ground-Launched Cruise Missile), 87, 90, 116–17, 119, 136–40

ICBM (Intercontinental Ballistic Missile): deployments, 84; heavy, 146, 148, 155; mobile, 84, 86, 146–47, 148; reduced reliance on, 85, 144; warhead ceilings, 148. *See also* missiles; SS-18; survivability
ideology. *See* class conflict
imperialism, 57, 59, 67. *See also* capitalism
IRM (Intermediate-Range Missile), 88, 116–19, 136–41
ISRM Treaty (Intermediate- and Short-Range Missiles), 88, 139–40; consequences, 118–19; negotiations, 138–39; savings from, 39. *See also* zero option
INF (Intermediate-range Nuclear Forces), 88; negotiations, 116, 136–37, 139; walkout, 100, 103
international system, 2–4, 99, 164
Izyumov, Alexei, 52, 58

Japan, 56, 107, 108

Karaganov, Sergei, 115, 118, 119
Karpov, Viktor, 21
KGB, 20, 26 n.7
Kiryan, Mikhail, 80
Kohl, Helmut, 122, 124, 131 n.57
Kokoshin, Andrei, 82, 86, 87, 105
Konovalev, Anatoli, 20
Kortunov, Andrei, 52, 54, 58, 59
Kozyrev, Andrei, 50
Kunadze, Georgi, 66

Lance missile, 124, 126, 142
launch-on-warning, 81
leadership change, 12, 15, 25
Ligachev, Yegor, 14, 15, 53

machine-building, 29–31, 33, 34, 38, 42–43
Maksimov, Yuri, 18, 77
Medvedev, Vadim, 51
Melville, Andrei, 55
military doctrine: review, 75; war prevention, 49
military expenditures. *See* CIA estimates, Soviet military expenditures
military high command, 17–20; parity, 67; stability, 86; strategic arms cuts, 63, 149; threat assessment, 60; TNW, 92; triad, 145; war fighting, 75, 86; war prevention, 49
Military-Industrial Commission, 20, 26 n.7
military-industrial complex. *See* defense complex
military modernists, 18–19, 37
military power, 161; economic basis, 54; reliance on, 60, 159; value, 2–3, 53, 62–63
military reform, 19, 41, 42, 161, 162
military resources shifted to civilian sector, 39–40, 54, 159
missiles: ballistic, 86–87, 157 n.26; cruise, 86, 143, 144, 147; Europe, 135; heavy, 157 n.26; land-based, 143, 148; MIRVed, 157 n.18; procurement, 38; single- warhead, 163; tactical, 140–41, 142–43, 156–57 n.15. *See also* ALCM; GLCM; ICBM; IRM; SLBM; SLCM; SRM; SS-18; SS-20; SS-24; SS-25
MX missile, 77, 146–47, 149
Moiseyev, Mikhail, 18, 19, 39; defense cuts, 67; parity, 66; threat from West, 59, 60, 63

MIRV. *See* warhead

NATO, 68, 113, 115–27; TNW, 142, 155, 156 n.15, 163–64; threat from, 59, 60, 63, 80; use of nuclear weapons, 87, 89–92
navy, 55, 146
negotiations, 101, 102
new political thinking, 9, 14, 47–68, 102, 112, 116, 162
no-first-use, 75–76, 79, 146
nuclear arsenals: cuts, 63–67, 83, 87, 144; restructuring, 93, 154, 159; uility, 55
nuclear balance, 92, 93, 101, 117, 159
nuclear strategy, 79–83, 149, 162. *See also* military doctrine; no-first-use; targeting
NST (Nuclear and Space Talks), 21, 137–38, 146, 152–53
nuclear war: fighting, 81–82; limited, 90, 91, 140, 141; risks, 92, 109; victory, 48–49, 56, 76, 80–81, 105
Nunn, Sam, 110

parity, 76, 77, 119, 159; conventional arms, 125; cost, 36–37; Europe, 87, 117, 139; preserving, 66–67; utility, 54, 55, 64, 65
peace, 48–49, 63
perestroika, 3, 14, 37, 53, 111, 116. *See also* domestic reform
Perle, Richard, 106
Pershing-2, 87, 90, 116–17, 119, 136–37, 139
Politburo, 13–15, 17, 20, 24, 37; commission on political-military affairs, 13, 14, 19, 20, 22, 26 n.7

Ponomarev, Boris, 16
preemption, 82, 143, 146
Presidential Council, 17, 18, 19
Primakov, Yevgeni, 22–23, 54

Reagan, Ronald, 103, 105, 106, 110, 144
Reagan administration, 105–106, 110, 114, 146, 151, 155
reasonable sufficiency. *See* sufficiency
R&D, 29, 31, 38–39, 41–42, 107–108
research institutes. *See* Academy of Sciences
retaliation, 76, 77, 79, 83; BMD, 77, 150, 162; bombers, 85; cruise missiles, 143; strategy, 79–81
Rogov, Sergei, 106, 108
Ryzhkov, Nikolai, 37, 40

Sagdeyev, Roald, 38
second strike. *See* retaliation
scientists, 20, 23, 107, 108
scientific-technological revolution, 2, 49, 50, 57, 60, 67, 161
SDI (Strategic Defense Initiative): cost, 106–8; countermeasures, 77–78; European attitude, 114–15; negotiations, 138, 150–55, 163; threat, 77, 108–9; U.S. policy, 109–112
security aims, 3–5, 6, 160–61. *See also* new political thinking
Semeyko, Lev, 76
Shabanov, Vitali, 41–42
Silayev, Ivan, 31
Shcherbytsky, Volodymyr, 14, 15
Shevardnadze, Eduard, 13, 32, 53, 61, 102; ABM, 152; class struggle, 50; common European home, 23–24; concessions, 155–56; diplomacy, 60, 62; Foreign Ministry, 12, 20, 21; ISRM, 138, 139, 140, 141; NATO, 122, 126; START, 144, 147, 148; TNW, 126, 142, 143, 156 n.15
SLCM (Sea-Launched Cruise Missile), 84, 85, 147–48, 157 n.21
SRM (Short-Range Missile), 88, 89, 90–91, 140–42, 155. *See also* zero option, double
Shultz, George, 106
socialism, 49–53, 61, 102
Sokolov, Sergei, 15, 17, 63, 64
space-based defenses, 1, 7. *See also* ABM; BMD
stability: 3, 161, 162; arms control, 62, 135, 159, 160; arms race, 101; BMD, 76, 109; Europe, 87, 91, 111, 120, 127; force restructuring, 84–87; military conditions, 81–82; political, 93, 99; strategic arms cuts, 66, 143, 145, 149–50
Starodubov, Viktor, 21
stealth technology, 77, 108
SALT II (Strategic Arms Limitation Treaty), 1, 139, 144
START (Strategic Arms Reduction Talks), 83, 135, 143–49, 157 nn.18, 26; follow-on negotiations, 87, 139, 149–50, 163; link to ABM Treaty, 150–53
Strategic Missile Forces, 22, 42, 84
SLBM (Submarine-Launched Ballistic Missile), 84, 86, 148, 157 n.26, 163
SNVD (Strategic Nuclear Delivery Vehicle), 145, 148, 157 n.18
Sturua, Georgi, 100, 102, 103
submarines, 84–85, 146, 147

sufficiency, 19, 24, 65–66
summit meetings: Geneva (1985), 103, 105; Reykjavik (1986), 18, 106, 110, 141, 145–47, 151; Washington (1987), 18, 147, 151, 157 n.26; Moscow (1988), 152; Malta (1989), 111; Washington (1990), 111–12, 148, 150, 152–53
Supreme Soviet, 11, 16, 17, 20, 21–22, 112; Defense Committee, 21–22, 23, 43, 162; International Affairs Committee, 21–22, 23
SS–18, 84, 146
SS–20, 87–90, 116, 136–40, 155
SS–24, 84, 148, 149, 157 n.24
SS–25, 84, 86
survivability, 77, 82, 83, 135, 150; submarines, 84, 86; TNW, 92; triad, 85

TASM (Tactical Air-to-Surface Missile), 125, 127
TNW (Tactical Nuclear Weapons), 88, 89; military role, 90–92; negotiations, 123, 125–26, 140–43; NATO approach, 124–27, 163–64; unilateral cuts, 156–57 n.15
targeting: change in priorities, 162; counterforce, 79–81, 149, 163; countervalue, 81; disagreements over, 75, 83; weapon systems, 84–87
technology, 3, 31, 50–51, 101; civilian sector, 38, 41, 43, 54, 107; United States, 64, 65; weaponry, 4, 18–19, 35, 41–42
Third World, 4, 51–52, 61, 104
threat to USSR, 56–60, 63, 66, 112, 160
throw-weight, 148

trade, 111–12, 132 n.75, 137–38
triad, 83, 85, 144–45, 148, 163

unilateral arms reductions, 66, 125, 143, 156–57 n.15
United States: arms control, 62, 66–67, 87, 99, 154–56, 162; Congress, 99, 106, 109, 110, 153–54; economy, 36–37, 56; ISRM, 136, 138, 140; nuclear guarantees to NATO allies, 117–20, 124–25, 127; nuclear presence in Europe, 123, 163–64; relations with USSR, 102–105, 111–12; relations with Western Europe, 113–15; Republicans, 99, 105, 109, 110; response to Soviet expansion, 58–59; Soviet analysis of, 101; space weapons talks, 150–54, 163; START, 145–50, 163; threat from, 57, 60, 63, 65; TNW, 142–43; vulnerability, 76–77; weapons, 85, 93. *See also* Reagan administration
Ustinov, Dmitri, 17

Velikhov, Yevgeni, 23
verification, 8, 112, 140, 143, 147
Vorontsov, Yuli, 21

war, danger of, 56–57, 59
warhead: ceilings, 144, 145, 148; concentration, 82, 86, 87, 145, 150, 157 n.26; proliferation, 84–85, 143; reduction, 149
Warsaw Pact, 24, 52–53, 80, 126, 163–64; arms reductions, 125–26, 141
weaponry, 5; cost of production, 35, 41–42, 43; procurement, 34, 36, 38; technology, 42, 54–55

Weinberger, Caspar, 106
West: arms control, 4, 104; assistance, 160, 164; interaction with, 51, 100; interests, 62, 155; response to Soviet policy, 58–59, 61–62; rivalry, 49–50, 52, 54; suspicion of, 59, 62–63, 66–67. *See also* East-West cooperation
Western Europe: cooperation with USSR, 113–14, 118–19; ISRM, 117–18, 137–38, 140; military integration, 119–20; relations with United States, 113–15; security arrangements, 117–19; Soviet policy towards, 112. *See also* United States, nuclear guarantees to NATO allies; United States, nuclear presence in Europe

Yakovlev, Aleksandr, 13, 16, 24, 26 n.7, 51, 113
Yazov, Dmitri, 15, 17, 18, 105; deterrence, 77, 80–81; ISRM Treaty, 140; weaponry, 42, 65; West, 59, 60, 66–67

Zaikov, Lev, 19, 26 n.7
zero option, 88, 117, 139–40, 154, 155; double, 15, 88, 124, 140–42, 155; third, 88–89, 124, 127, 142
Zhurkin, Vitali, 57, 87; common European home, 23–24, 120–21; Pershing-2, 90; sufficiency, 65, 66; war, 56–57

ABOUT THE AUTHOR

DANIEL CALINGAERT holds a B.A. in international relations from Tufts University and a Master's degree in Soviet studies from Oxford University. He is completing a doctoral dissertation at Oxford on Soviet nuclear arms control policy.